THE ATHENIAN CALENDAR
IN THE FIFTH CENTURY

———

BENJAMIN DEAN MERITT

THE
ATHENIAN CALENDAR
IN THE FIFTH CENTURY

BASED ON A STUDY OF THE DETAILED ACCOUNTS OF MONEY
BORROWED BY THE ATHENIAN STATE

I.G. I^2, 324

BY

BENJAMIN DEAN MERITT

Select Bibliographies Reprint Series

BOOKS FOR LIBRARIES PRESS
FREEPORT, NEW YORK

First Published 1928
Reprinted 1969

LIBRARY OF CONGRESS CATALOG CARD NUMBER:
74-75510

PRINTED IN THE UNITED STATES OF AMERICA

TO

EDWARD CAPPS

THIS BOOK

IS AFFECTIONATELY DEDICATED

TABLE OF CONTENTS

PLATE I

I.G. I², 324 — 426/5–423/2 B.C.

PREFACE

The study which is presented in this volume was begun in 1925 when I first approached the problem of determining the amounts of principal and interest recorded in the accounts of state expenditures for the year 426-5 B. C. (*I. G.* I², 324). It was soon apparent that no one part of the inscription could be studied independently, and during the summer of 1925 exact copies of all the known fragments were made, and the scope of the work was extended. It was not until 1927, however, that the opportunity presented itself for consistent work with the stones themselves in the Epigraphical Museum at Athens. I am under the greatest obligation to Dr. Basileios Leonardos, the Director of the Museum, for placing at my disposal every possible facility in the course of this investigation and for his permission to make public the results of the study.

One by one the various fragments were assigned to their proper places in the inscription. The restoration of the text depends largely on mathematical calculations, and in so far as this is true it is, I believe, mathematically certain. One fundamental assumption has been made in the calculations which involve maxima and minima, viz., that the length of a prytany may have been as much as forty days or as little as thirty-three days. No one who has studied the problems of the Athenian calendar, I am sure, will consider these limits too conservative.

I wish here to acknowledge my indebtedness to Mr. Jotham Johnson, Fellow of the American School of Classical Studies, for his suggestions relative to the tables presented in the text for the computation of interest, and to Miss Hazel Hansen for her assistance in reading the manuscript in proof and in preparing the index. I wish also to express my gratitude to Mr. H. T. Wade-Gery of Oxford, to Dr. Johannes Kirchner of Berlin, and to Dr. Allen B. West of the University of Cincinnati for many helpful suggestions. I am also under obligation to Dr. H. H. Powers, President of the Bureau of University Travel, and Hon. Frederick W. Griffith of Palmyra, N. Y., for constant interest and assistance in making this study possible, and to Dr. Edward Capps, whose name appears on the page of dedication.

Athens, Greece. April 4, 1928.

B. D. MERITT

THE ATHENIAN CALENDAR

CHAPTER I

INTRODUCTION

It was the good fortune of the American School of Classical Studies to find, during excavations in the Erechtheum in 1914, several small pieces of the highly interesting and important inscription from the fifth century which gives to us the detailed accounts of money borrowed by the state from Athena Polias, Athena Nike, Hermes, and the «Other Gods», during the quadrennium from 426 to 422 B.C. Several of these small pieces were transcribed by Mr. B. H. Hill and copies of the transcriptions were sent to Hiller von Gaertringen for publication in the *Editio Minor* of the *Corpus,* Vol. I. These fragments appear there as frgs. *i, k, l, m,* and *n* of *I. G.* I², 324. Of these, fragment *i* was assigned to its correct position in the inscription by Bannier, and it is given in the *Corpus* according to his designation.

One fragment, to which I shall refer for convenience as frg. *o,* is published separately in the *Corpus* as *I. G.* I², 306, although it clearly belongs to this inscription and in fact makes a direct join with frg. *n.*

We must here discuss these small fragments again, together with one other piece as yet unpublished which was found at the same place and at the same time. I have called this new piece frg. *p.* There are also in the Epigraphical Museum two other small pieces of the stone on which this inscription was cut. They bear no letters, but they preserve part of the characteristic bevelled surface which was cut on both sides of the stone by some mediaeval workman.

The following table shows the inventory numbers by which the various fragments of *I.G.* I², 324, old and new, are designated in the Epigraphical Museum at Athens.

Frgs. $a+b+c+e+f+g$ = EM 6741

Frg. d = EM 6741a

Frg. h = Lost

Frg. i = EM 12355

Frg. k = EM 12357

Frg. l = EM 12363

Frg. m = EM 12360

Frg. n = EM 12358

Frg. o = *I. G.* I² 306 = EM 12359

Frg. p = EM 12362

Two uninscribed pieces = EM 12355a and EM 12355b.

It has been possible to place definitely every one of the new fragments mentioned above and at the same time to determine the relative positions of the two large fragments, b and f, from the upper and lower sections of the stone. Also it may be observed that frg. d, which has been known for many years, makes a direct join with frg. f. In many places the text of the document must be in large part rewritten, and in the following pages the attempt is made to justify the text which appears in Plate II at the end of this book.

The problems of the Athenian calendar are inevitably involved in any attempt to restore the inscription, but I have first dealt mainly with the problems offered by the document itself, leaving till the latter part of the study a discussion of the correspondences between the civil and the senatorial calendars. In the following pages the civil year will always be understood to mean the year of the twelve Attic months from Hekatombaeon to Skirophorion, and the senatorial year the year of the ten prytanies from Pryt. I, 1 to Pryt. X, *ultimo*.

CHAPTER II

THE NEW FRAGMENTS

The first problem is that of establishing the text of the new fragments. It will be noticed that frgs. $k+l+m$ are given in the *Corpus* as *inter se contigua*. As a matter of fact there is no connection between these several pieces, and the restorations now proposed must be changed. Frg. l makes a direct join with frg. i in such a way that the combined text of the two fragments reads as follows:

(See Photograph I)

```
— — Ἀθεν]αίας ἐν τοῖ[ς] τέ[τταρσιν — ·
— — κεφά]λαιον τόκο χσύμπαν[τος — —
— — — — Δ]ⲘΤΤΤΧΧΧⲘΗΗΗΗΔΔΔΠ[ — —
— — — πρ]υτανευόσες τετάρτε[ι τε͂ς — — —
— — τόκος] τούτοις ἐ[γ]ένετο Η[ — — — —
— — ἐλογίσα]ντο [ℎοι] λογιστ[αὶ — — — —
— — — — — Παναθέν]αια[ — — — — —
```

Aside from the fact that frg. l actually joins frg. i the restoration of the *Corpus* cannot be correct, because the word ἐ]λογίσ[αντο in line 72 necessitates an *alpha* where the *tau* of λογισταί is perfectly preserved on the stone. Also in line 71 the interest accrued is given as an amount larger than the sum of the principal on which it was reckoned. With frg. i and frg. l now joined together we know that this broken numeral, of which the initial figure Η alone is preserved, represents the interest which was reckoned on the loan from Athena Nike. *Cf. I. G.* I², 324, line 53. It will appear later that the amount of this principal was six talents (ⲘΤ).

Fragment *n* is to be joined with frg. *o,* as shown in Photograph II. The contact surface between the two stones is not large but it is none the less certain. The combined inscriptions read as follows:

(See Photograph II)

```
– – – – – ε̣ν – – – – – – – – – – – – – –
– – παρέδοσ]αν h[οι ταμίαι – – – – – – – –
– – – – – χ]ρεμάτο[ν – – – – – – – – – –
– – – – – – ]ος πρõτ[ος ἐγραμμάτευε – – –
– – – – – – ]νος ὀγ[ – – – – – – – – – –
Ἀρτέμιδος Ἀγρ]οτέρα[ς – – – – – – – – – –
– – – – – – – ]ΗⱭΔ[ – – – – – – – – – – –
– – – – – ]ΙΙ τό[κος τούτο – – – – – – – –
Ποσειδõν]ος ἐπὶ Σο[υνίοι – – – – – – – – –
– – τόκο]ς τούτο [ – – – – – – – – – – – –
```

Photograph I. Frgs. *i+l.*

I have given above only so much of the restoration as is apparent at first glance. We have the opening lines of the record of one of the payments made by the treasurers of the Other Gods, for the characteristic lines – – παρέδοσ]αν h[οι ταμίαι – – – and – – –]ος πρō̄τ[ος ἐγραμμάτευε – – – show that the first part of the passage quoted here belongs in fact to a preamble, and the mention made of Artemis Agrotera and Poseidon at Sunium indicates that the payment was made from the treasure of the Other Gods.

It is certain, however, that in the inscription with which we have to deal only two payments were made from this treasure, and that both of these fell in the year

Photograph II. Frgs. *n* + *o*.

423-2 B.C. (*Cf.* Plate II, lines 55, 75, 77, 94-96). The various lines of frgs. *n* + *o* find their counterpart in the preamble and opening portion of the record of the second payment. It follows, therefore, that frgs. *n* + *o* themselves belong to the beginning of the record of the first payment. It is possible, with the help of the inevitable restorations in lines 54 and 55 to give to frgs. *n* + *o* a definite place in the inscription. Fragment *m* is to be placed in connection with frg. *o,* although there is no direct join between them, and the readings are given in lines 59 and 60. For divergences from the text of the *Corpus,* see Photograph III. With frgs. *m, n,* and *o* in their proper relation to fragments *i, l, c,* and *b,* lines 54 ff. may now be read as follows:

54   [τάδε ἐλογίσα]ντο [hοι] λογιστ[αὶ ὀφελόμ]εν[α τοῖς ἄλλοις θεοῖς
           ἐν τοῖς τέττ]αρσιν ἔτ[εσιν ἐκ Παν]-

55   [αθεναίον ἐς Παναθέν]αια [τάδε (?) παρέδοσ]αν h[οι ταμίαι τõν
           ἄλλον θεõν Γόργο]ινος Ο[ἰνείδο Ἰκαρι]-

56   [εὺς καὶ χσυνάρχοντες ἐκ τõν hεκάστο χ]ρεμάτο[ν hελλενοταμίαις
           καὶ στρατ]εγοῖς [_ 4 or 5 _ καὶ χσυ]-

57   [νάρχοσιν ἐπὶ τῆς βολῆς hῆι Δεμέτρι]ος πρõτ[ος ἐγραμμάτευε
           ἐπὶ τῆς Ἀκαμαντ]ίδ[ος (?) πρυτανείας]

58   [. . . 6? . . . πρυτανευόσες . . . . . 11? . . . . .]νος ὀγ[δόει — — —]

59   [. . . . . 17 . . . . Ἀρ]τέμι[δος Ἀγρ]οτέρα[ς — — — — —]

60   [. . . . . 18 . . . . τό]κος τ[ούτο . .]ΗΠΔ[— — — —]

61   [. . . . . 29 . . . .]ΙΙ τό[κος τούτο — — —]

62   [. . . . . 17 . . . . Ποσειδõν]ος ἐπὶ Σο[υνίοι — — — — —]

63   [. . . . . 21 . . . . τόκο]ς το[ύτο — — — — — — —]

Line 54 reads substantially as it is now given in the *Corpus,* for it has only been necessary to interchange the positions of the words ὀφελόμενα and τοῖς ἄλλοις θεοῖς to make the restoration conform with the letters preserved in the first line of

Photograph III, Frg. *m.*

frg. *o.* These letters are clearly EN, although only the right tip of the lower horizontal stroke of the *epsilon* is still preserved on the stone. The stone is fractured just above the *nu* as well, but portions of all three strokes may still be discerned. The right vertical stroke has left only a trace, but the diagonal bar, which is preserved along the edge of the stone, rises so high on the left vertical bar that the letter can only have been a *nu.*

In line 55 notice that the uninscribed space indicated in the *Corpus* after the word Παναθέναια must be omitted, in order that the final letters of this word (αια) may fall under the letters λογ above as shown in Photograph I. The line is made of proper length by including the *nu*-movable with the word ἔτεσιν in line 54.

The restorations in line 56 are not certain and are offered merely by way of suggestion.

In line 57 appears the name of the secretary of the senate, Δεμέτριος, without the demotic, although the name appears above in line 37 as Δεμέτριος Κολλυτεύς. On account of the letter spaces the prytanizing tribe must be restored either as Ἀκαμαντίς or Πανδιονίς. The two letters ΙΔ of the genitive ending are preserved on the stone in frg. c.

Line 58 offers something really new and of the greatest interest, for we have here the evidence of date by month. Normally, throughout *I. G.* I², 324, the dates on which payments were made from the sacred treasures are given only by the day of the prytany, *i. e.,* by the senatorial calendar. We have here not only the date by prytany, but also the date by the month of the civil year — and we should have, if we could restore the line with certainty, a cross-reference between the civil and the senatorial year which might help in solving the complicated problem of the Athenian calendar in the fifth century. Without further evidence, however, it is impossible to restore the date by prytany in line 58, and for the moment we must postpone our study of these lines.

We have, nevertheless, the knowledge that at least in the preamble of the record of the first payment of money from the treasure of the Other Gods the date was given twice, once by the civil year and once by the senatorial year. The formulae of date follow, in fact, in this order:

1. ἐπὶ τὲς — — — ίδος πρυτανείας — — — πρυτανευόσες
2. Date by civil month
3. Date by prytany

We have every reason to expect that the same system of dating was followed in the preamble of the second payment as well, and an examination of the stone shows this to be the case.

In lines 83-84 of the *Corpus* we read as follows:

ἐπὶ τὲς Λεοντίδος πρυτανείας δεκάτε[ς πρυτανευόσες
. . . . .¹⁵ . . . .]σοειοθ[. . .⁷ . . . εἰ]κοστὲι τὲς
πρυτανείας.

These lines repeat the rubrics which appeared in the date of the first payment, and in the same order. Fortunately the stone is well enough preserved so that we may restore with certainty both the name and the date of the month. I have examined the stone in Athens carefully and am convinced that the doubtful *sigma* in line 84 is in reality a *delta*. The word is ὀγ]δόει. The name of the month to be restored before it is Σκιροφοριῶνος, which falls into the space available on the stone and corresponds well with the date as given in the tenth prytany. The other word belonging to the date (following ὀγδόει) is to be restored as φθ[ίνοντος]. We have in these two lines

2

a very important epigraphical check between the senatorial and the civil calendars in the fifth century — and we may now be certain that in the year 423-2 B.C. the date Σκιροφοριῶνος ὀγδόε φθίνοντος of the civil calendar was the same as the date εἰκοστὲ τες (δεκάτες) πρυτανείας of the senatorial calendar.

I should notice here Kubicki's reading of the letters which I have interpreted as part of the words ὀγδόει φθίνοντος. He has given the line in question with the following restoration:

στρατεγοῖς hοι ἔχ]σο εἰόθ[ασι πλεν

I am quite certain, however, that the first doubtful letter is not a *sigma,* but *delta*. Earlier editors have professed to see on the stone here only the corner of an angular letter (*cf.* Rangabé, *Rev. Arch.* 1845, p. 324) and this corner of the letter is still on the stone today in such a position that it can be completed only as the letter *delta*. Pittakys ('Εφ. 'Αρχ. no. 1351) and Velsen (*cf.* Boeckh's *Kleine Schriften*, Vol. VI, p. 221) omit the letter entirely from their copies. Unfortunately the stone has been so broken since its discovery that the letter which I have given as *phi* is only partially preserved. The *theta* is entirely gone. The *phi*, however, is preserved in such a way as to preclude the possibility of its having been a normally shaped *omicron*, although it has always been read as such. The left rounding of the letter is still on the stone, but it is a depressed oval-shaped rounding, like that of the letter *phi*, not like that of the letter *omicron*. And, of more significance still, the stroke of the rounding stops short of the upper centre, so that if the letter were really an *omicron* there must have been a space of perhaps a millimeter at the top where the circle did not close. I mention this because it shows that in any case the letter was never completely cut. And I think a stonemason would be more apt to leave unfinished a *phi* than an *omicron*, because of the greater danger of splitting away the surface of the stone when the vertical bar of the *phi* should be added, if the stone at that point happened to be especially friable. We have from this same inscription an example of such an unfinished *phi* in the line 'Αφροδίτες ἐν hιππολυ[τείοι of frg. *k,* which may be seen in Photograph V. Here the circle was not closed at the top, and the vertical bar was not extended across the surface of the stone within the circle.

Since those editors who saw the stone, however, before it was broken away are agreed in reading the letter as *omicron*, I assume that even these vertical bars outside the circle were not added in this instance, but that the letter appeared on the stone merely as a depressed oval-shaped rounding, slightly open at the top. Examples of the letter *phi* with the vertical bar omitted are not extremely rare, and I may cite as one instance of approximately the same date the initial *phi* of the word φσεφισαμέν[ο in *I. G.* I², 302, line 27, where the letters which actually appéar on the stone are οσεφισαμέν[ο.

The fact that the day Σκιροφοριῶνος ὀγδόε φθίνοντος coincided with the day εἰκοστὲ τὲς (δεκάτες) πρυτανείας in the year 423-2 B.C. means that the last day of the last prytany fell early in the month of Hekatombaeon of the ensuing civil year. We may expect difficulty, however, in determining the exact correspondences, because the month Skirophorion may be either full or hollow and we have no indication as yet as to the length of the last prytany. According to the calculations of Keil (*cf.* *Hermes*, XXIX, 1894, p. 358) the last day of the last prytany fell on the sixth day of Hekatombaeon, but we shall soon see that this is not true and also that the correction suggested in the *Corpus* (*Editio Minor*, Vol. I, p. 154), making the last day of the tenth prytany fall on the fourth day of Hekatombaeon, is likewise impossible.

It is now generally agreed that throughout this inscription interest was reckoned on the various payments of money down to the Greater Panathenaic festival of the year 422 B.C. A summary of the prevailing view is given in the commentary in the *Corpus* (p. 155), where it is demonstrated that interest was reckoned for 1464 days for the duration of the whole four year period from the summer of 426 to the summer of 422. I should like to point, however, to one curious anomaly in the present system of reckoning. It is assumed that the first day for which interest in this quadrennium was computed was the first day of Pryt. I in the year 426-5 (*Corpus, Editio Minor*, Vol. I, p. 153 and table p. 154) and at the same time it is assumed that the interest period ran, not to the last day of the year 423-2, but to the Panathenaea of the year 422.

The most apparent interpretation of our epigraphical evidence is that the records covered the period from Panathenaea to Panathenaea. It will suffice to quote the well known lines from *I.G.* I², 91 which deal with the establishment of the board of treasurers of the Other Gods: καὶ ἐκ Παναθεναίον ἐς Παναθέναια τὸλ λόγον διδόντον καθάπερ hοι τὰ τὲς Ἀθεναίας τ[α]μιεύοντες and the several instances in this very inscription where mention is made of the reckoning from Panathenaea to Panathenaea.

1. lines 1-2: [τάδε ἐλογίσαντ]ο hοι λογιστα[ὶ ἐν τοῖς τέτ]ταρσιν ἔτεσιν ἐκ Παναθεναίον ἐς [Παναθέναια ὀφελόμενα]

2. lines 48-49: κεφάλαι[ον ἀν]αλόματος χσ[ύμπαντος Ἀθεν]αίας ἐν τοῖ[ς] τέ[τταρσιν ἔ]τεσιν ἐκ Παναθεναίον ἐς Παναθέν[αια   —]

3. lines 50-51: κεφά]λαιον τόκο χσύμπαν[τος Ἀθε]ναίας ἐν τοῖς τέτταρσιν ἔτεσιν ἐ[κ Παν]αθεναίον ἐς Πα[ναθέναια   — —]

4. lines 54 - 55: [τάδε ἐλογίσα]ντο [hοι] λογιστ[αὶ ὀφελόμ]εν[α τοῖς ἄλλοις θεοῖς ἐν τοῖς τέττ]αρσιν ἔτ[εσιν ἐκ Παναθεναίον ἐς Παναθέν]αια.

August Boeckh, and those who followed his principle of restoration (cf. *Kleine Schriften*, Vol. VI, pp. 96 ff.), reckoned the four years of the civil calendar in fixing the quadrennium from 426 to 422. There are two other possible interpretations which are in themselves consistent, i. e., the quadrennium of the senatorial calendar and the quadrennium of the Panathenaic interval. I give a summary below of possible first and last dates for the reckoning of interest.

1. Hekatombaeon 1, 426-5   to   Skirophorion 29-30, 423-2
2. Panathenaea of 426   to   Panathenaea of 422
3. Prytany I, 1, 426-5   to   Prytany X, *ultimo*, 423-2

My objection to the system which has now found acceptance is that it is not consistent in itself. The first day for the reckoning of interest follows scheme 3, but the last day for the reckoning of interest follows scheme 2. And if one is to assume that interest was reckoned from Panathenaea to Panathenaea the only way of obviating this inconsistency is to assume that Pryt. I, 1 in 426-5 coincided with the date of the Panathenaic festival of that year. This is at variance with Keil's table not only in fact but also in theory.

We must suppose also, if we accept the current doctrine, that interest during the quadrennium from 430 to 426 was reckoned down to the Panathenaic festival of the year 426. According to Keil's table, as corrected in the *Corpus* (p. 154) this assumption means that interest from Hekatombaeon 11 to the Panathenaea in 426 was being reckoned twice, once by the *logistae* from 430 to 426 and again by the *logistae* from 426 to 422. I urge that this is impossible.

We are fortunate, however, in having in our inscription sufficient evidence to make possible a solution of the difficulty, and to this evidence we must now turn our attention.

In lines 103-105 (cf. Plate II) Kubicki has restored the sum total of money spent from the treasure of the Other Gods in the seven years from 433 to 426 as follows:[1] πε]ντακοσίοις ταλάντοις διακοσίοις τ[αλάντοις ηεχσέχοντα ταλάντοι]ς ηὲχς ταλ[άντοις χιλίαις ἐνενέχοντα δραχμαῖς πέντε δραχ[μαῖς πέντε ὀβολοῖς, and the interest which this amount drew in 1464 days was [Δ]ΔΔ⊓ΤΤΧΧΗΗΗΔΔΔ⊓ΗΗΙΙC. The significant figures of this latter sum are all preserved, and the restoration of the initial Δ is certain. The rate of interest was the same as that used throughout the inscription: Five talents in one day yields one drachma.

---

[1] Kubicki, Das Schaltjahr der grossen Rechnungs-Urkunde IG I 273, *Progr. Ratibor*, 1885, p. 26.

We may be certain therefore that the rate of interest at this time which applied to moneys borrowed from the Other Gods was the same as the rate which applied to moneys borrowed from Athena. We have only to use this rate of interest and to compute from the preserved items of the second payment of the Other Gods the number of days for which the payment was outstanding.

In line 85 (cf. Plate II) the sum of TXⱲHHΔΔΔΔⱤⱵⱵⱵ was drawn from the treasure of Hephaestus and the interest amounted to ⱵⱵⱵⱵIIC. The number of days for which the sum was outstanding is exactly 17. Reckon as follows:

TXⱲ	in one day yields	$1 \frac{1}{2}$ obols
HHΔΔΔΔⱤⱵⱵⱵ (app. HHⱲ)	in one day yields	$\frac{1}{20}$ obol
TXⱲHHΔΔΔΔⱤⱵⱵⱵ	in one day yields	$1 \frac{11}{20}$ obols
TXⱲHHΔΔΔΔⱤⱵⱵⱵ	in 17 days yields	$26 \frac{7}{20}$ obols

As nearly as this amount of interest can be expressed in Greek monetary signs, it reads ⱵⱵⱵⱵIIC, which is the numeral we have preserved on the stone.

In line 88 (cf. Plate II) the amount of the principal and the amount of the interest are again both preserved. The sum of XXXHHHHΔⱤⱵⱵⱵI borrowed from Athena in Pallenis yielded ⱵIIIIIC as interest, and the number of days again appears as 17. The amount may be reckoned as follows:

XXⱲ	in one day yields	$\frac{1}{2}$ obol
ⱲHHHHΔⱤⱵⱵⱵI	in one day yields	$\frac{3}{16}$ obol
XXXHHHHΔⱤⱵⱵⱵI	in one day yields	$\frac{11}{16}$ obol
XXXHHHHΔⱤⱵⱵⱵI	in 17 days yields	$11 \frac{11}{16}$ obols

The calculation is a trifle high, because $\frac{3}{16}$ obol per day is actually the interest on $937 \frac{1}{2}$ Dr., rather than on $918 \frac{1}{6}$ Dr. But with this in mind we may write the amount of interest as nearly as it can be expressed in Greek monetary signs as ⱵIIIIIC, and this is the numeral which is preserved on the stone.

This same process may be followed in the case of the payment in line 87 (cf. Plate II) from the treasure belonging to Herakles in Kynosarges. The principal of 80 Dr. yields $\frac{1}{4}$ obol in 15 days. In 17 days we must concede the benefit of the fraction to the god, and the closest approximation possible in the Greek numerical signs is C. This number actually appears on the stone.

In line 91, as the text is given in the *Corpus* (cf. line 86, Plate II), there is an apparent exception to the regular rate of interest, for while we have just seen that 80 Dr. yielded $\frac{1}{2}$ obol as interest, we find here the statement that 71 Dr. yields

$1\frac{3}{4}$ obols as interest. The amount of the principal is mistakenly given, however, as may be readily ascertained by a reference to the majuscule text of the first edition of the *Corpus* (*I. G.* I, 273, p. 145, line 18) or by reference to the stone in Athens, where the initial numeral ⊩ is perfectly preserved. We have, in fact, to reckon interest on a principal of 521 Dr., as follows:

⊩	in one day yields	$\frac{1}{10}$ obol
ΔΔ⊢ (ΔΔ)	in one day yields	$\frac{1}{240}$ obol
⊩ΔΔ⊢	in one day yields	$\frac{25}{240}$ obols
⊩ΔΔ⊢	in 17 days yields	$1\frac{3}{4}$ obols

Expressed in Greek numerical signs, this numeral is ΙϹϽ, which we have actually preserved on the stone.

These are the only payments where the amount of the principal and the amount of the interest are both preserved, and they give to us the indisputable proof that the loans were outstanding for 17 days from the date of payment to the day when the interest was calculated. This observation was made by Boeckh, and was followed by Kirchhoff in his edition of the inscription in the first volume of the *Corpus Inscriptionum Atticarum* (*I.G.* I, 273). I repeat it here because no mention is made of the 17 day period in the *Editio Minor* of the *Corpus,* and yet it is of fundamental importance for an understanding of the inscription.

We may note further that all the other fragmentary numerals from line 79 to line 93 (*cf.* Plate II) may be restored to give the same rate of interest and the same period of time. And finally we observe that the sum total of all the separate amounts of principal from the individual treasuries yields in 17 days the amount of interest which we find recorded in our inscription. This amount is preserved entire in line 95 as ⊠ΔΔΔ⊢⊢, and the amount of the principal (line 94) is ΔΔΤΤΤ⊠⊩ΗΗΗΗ[. . . . . .¹² . . . . .]. Of these twelve spaces which may have been occupied by numerical signs and which have not been restored in the *Corpus,* possibly two or three were left uninscribed. The numeral comes immediately before the item κεφάλαιον τόκο etc., and it is possible that there was more than one uninscribed space intervening.

A comparison of this numeral with the fragment still preserved of the sum total of the first payment (line 76) and with the combined sum total of both payments (line 96) shows that it must be restored as ΔΔΤΤΤ⊠⊩ΗΗΗΗ[⊠ΔΔΔΔΠ⊢⊢].

It must be noticed that the numerals of line 76 are so spaced on the stone that in reality there are seven spaces to the left and five spaces to the right of the figures still preserved (*cf.* Plate I). One of these latter five spaces must be left as the uninscribed space between the numeral and the words κεφάλαιον τόκο etc. which follow.

The principal of the first payment must now be added to the principal of the second payment to give the sum total, as follows:

line 76   ‒ ‒ ‒ ‒ ☒ΓΗΗ]ͰΗΓ[ΔΔΔΔ]

lines 94-95   ΔΔΤΤΤ☒ΓΗΗΗΗ[ΓΔΔΔΔΠͰͰͰ]

line 96   ‒ ΤΤ☒[ΓΗΗΗΗ]ΓΔΔΔΠͰͰͰ

We may leave for the time being the problem of restoring the initial figures in the numerals of lines 76 and 96, but so far as given above the restorations are certain. It is true that in line 96 I have restored only five figures where there is a *lacuna* of seven spaces, but the restoration is unique and admits of no alternative. Notice that the *stoichedon* order is not strictly followed after line 94 and that the individual figures for 500 Dr. and 100 Dr. may well have been broad enough to occupy the space (*cf.* Plate I).

The interest on the sum total of the second payment should be reckoned as follows:

ΔΔ	in one day yields	4 Dr.
ΤΤ☒Γ	in one day yields	$3\frac{1}{2}$ obols
ΤΗΗΗΗΓΔΔΔΔΠͰͰͰ	in one day yields	$1\frac{6}{20}$ obols
ΔΔΤΤΤ☒ΓΗΗΗΗΓΔΔΔΔΠͰͰͰ	in one day yields	4 Dr. $4\frac{4}{5}$ obols
ΔΔΤΤΤ☒ΓΗΗΗΗΓΔΔΔΔΠͰͰͰ	in 17 days yields	81 Dr. $3\frac{1}{2}$ obols

The amount of interest actually preserved on the stone is 82 Dr., so that our mathematical calculation has given a result which is too small by $2\frac{1}{2}$ obols. This is, however, just such a discrepancy as we should expect to find, for the λογισταί in Athens did not reckon the interest on the sum total of the payment but on the individual items of the payment. The sum total of the interest was obtained by adding the various separate items of interest thus calculated, and the amount of the error is greater, the greater the number of separate items included in the addition.

We have devoted some time to a restatement of the evidence for the fact that the second payment of moneys from the treasure of the Other Gods was outstanding for 17 days, because of its importance in our subsequent calculations. It solves, in fact, the problem of the *terminus ad quem* to which interest was reckoned, and the three possibilities mentioned above (p. 12) may now be considered again.

1. The final date was not at the end of the civil year, for Pryt. X, 20 — Skir 23, and 17 additional days would carry the terminus to Hekatombaeon 10.[1]

2. The final date was not at the Panathenaic festival, for the Panathenaea did not fall on or near the 10th day of Hekatombaeon.

3. The final date must have been the last day of the senatorial year.

This conclusion I consider unimpeachable and of primary importance. We must concede that the tenth prytany of the year 423-2 contained 36 days and that on the last day of this prytany the records of the quadrennium were closed. The 1464 days which comprised the quadrennium are then the days from Pryt. I, 1 in 426-5 to Pryt. X, 36 in 423-2. The quadrennium was measured by senatorial years, and this definition agrees well with our knowledge that the dates of payment throughout are recorded by the senatorial calendar (cf. Keil, *Hermes,* XXIX, 1894, p. 56).

We still have, however, the statement of the inscriptions (pp. 11-12 above) that the stewards of Athena's money and of the money of the Other Gods were to render their account from Panathenaea to Panathenaea, and that the λογισταί made their reckoning from Panathenaea to Panathenaea. No one questions the fact that the official year of the stewards of the sacred moneys was the Panathenaic year, and indeed we know from *I.G.* I², 295 that in 433-2 this year, which perhaps we may call the sacred year, was not coterminous with the senatorial year, for the board of treasurers was changed sometime between the 13th and the last day of the first prytany. It has also been generally recognized that the financial affairs of the state were conducted on the basis of the senatorial year (cf. Boeckh, *Kleine Schriften,* Vol. VI, p. 97; Keil, *Hermes,* 1894, pp. 55-56) in spite of the fact that the prescripts of our inscription refer to a reckoning in the four years «from Panathenaea to Panathenaea». We have in the evidence presented above, however, the first *proof* that this was the case, and we obtain thereby a valuable insight into the financial machinery of the Athenian state.[2]

. We obtain also a proof that the state records for individual years were not dated with extreme accuracy. For example, the accounts preserved in *I.G.* I², 324 are dated in three different ways: first by the Eponymous Archon, then by the first secretary of the senate, and finally by the treasurers of the Goddess. The year of the archon was not coterminous with the senatorial year, nor was the year of the treasurers

---

[1] We shall show below (Chap. VII) that the month of Skirophorion was full, and that Σκιροφοριῶνος ὀγδόε φθίνοντος was in fact the 23rd day of the month, not the 22nd, as would have been the case if Skirophorion were hollow. The point is of no consequence for the argument here.

[2] Nicklin arrived at approximately this same conclusion. *Cf.* The Attic Civil and Sacred Years, *Journal of Philology,* XXIV, 1896, pp. 54-82, especially p. 62.

coterminous with the senatorial year. These designations indicate clearly enough to which years the records belong, but they are not precise. We have found that the state records were kept on the basis of the year of the ten prytanies, and only the date as given by the first secretary of the senate is actually correct in its definition of limits. The period of four years from 426-5 to 423-2 is designated in our inscription as the period from Panathenaea to Panathenaea. When interpreted literally this phraseology is also inexact, for we know that the record of accounts ran from Pryt. I, 1 of 426-5 to Pryt. X, 36 of 423-2, not from Hek. 28 of 426 to Hek. 28 of 422. And yet to the Athenian the date as given from Panathenaea to Panathenaea caused no difficulty. It was merely the most convenient way of designating which sequence of four years was meant.

There is, therefore, no real inconsistency between the epigraphical evidence cited above and the conclusion we have reached that the official records of state were kept on the basis of the senatorial year. The stewards of the sacred moneys held office from Panathenaea to Panathenaea, entering or leaving office on the day of the yearly festival, and in so far as the quotation from *I.G.* I², 91 given above on p. 11 applies to them it is literally true. The treasurers were to stand their audit after their term of office, which is clearly defined, and the records of the treasurers must have covered this same period. One must be careful, however, to distinguish between the official records of the state (based on the senatorial year) and records of the treasurers as such (based on the year of the Panathenaic interval). We shall have occasion to recur to this point later.

An interesting problem in bookkeeping may now be raised as to how the record was kept by the state for a payment which may have been made from the sacred moneys (for state expense) during the first prytany of any given year when last year's books were closed, and before the Panathenaic festival when the new treasurers of the sacred moneys assumed their duties. I believe that an answer to this question can be given by the study of *I.G.* I², 324, lines 25-29.

We know, in fact, from *I.G.* I², 295 that such payments were made and that they were paid out by the old board of treasurers, who continued in office, of course, until the Panathenaea. They cannot have been entered on the state books which were closed on the last day of the preceding prytany, and they must have appeared as the first items in the records of state expense for the year following. But the custom of dating the state records not only by the first secretary of the senate but also by archon and treasurers of the Goddess led in consequence to a curious anomaly. To take a specific example, the accounts of the senatorial year 424-3 would be dated not only

3

by the first secretary of the senate, Epilykos (cf. Plate II, line 26), but also by the treasurers of the Goddess, Thucydides and his colleagues, while any payment made between Pryt. I, 1 and Hek. 28 would actually have been paid out by the board of treasurers over which Phokiades presided, and who were still in office during the first few weeks of the senatorial year.

This is the way in which I explain the fact that in *I.G.* I², 324, lines 25-29, the treasurers Thucydides and his colleagues are recorded as having made a payment to last year's hellenotamiae. Kirchhoff's explanation of this item is somewhat different (cf. *Editio Minor* of the *Corpus*. Vol. I, p. 155) for he believed that the treasurers of 424-3 were merely paying an amount which the treasurers of 425-4 had promised to pay. I object to this on several grounds, but primarily because it does not give a satisfactory date for the actual transfer of the money. If the old board of treasurers had promised to pay a certain sum — and had not made the transaction before they left office at the time of the Panathenaic festival—then the obligation of the new board of treasurers would be to the *new* board of hellenotamiae. In other words the responsibility of the old board of the hellenotamiae to receive the money ceased at the same time as the responsibility of the old board of treasurers to pay the money, and we still have left unexplained why the payment was made to last year's board.

To my mind, there is no doubt that the old board of hellenotamiae received this money from the old board of treasurers on the 26th day of the first prytany in the year 424-3. This date was before the Panathenaic festival, and the item could not be included in the record of state accounts for 425-4 because the books had been closed on the last day of the preceding prytany. It was consequently entered as the first item of expenditure in the succeeding year. This explains why the item is recorded under the stewardship of Thucydides, although the payment had been made under the stewardship of Phokiades. Interest of course was reckoned from the actual date of the payment, and the hellenotamiae by whom the money was received were the acting board at the time the payment was made. They are referred to here as the board of the previous year merely because the item paid to them had to be entered in the record of state expenses for 424-3.

I had reached the above conclusion before being able to prove by means of correspondences between the civil and the senatorial calendars that the payment must have fallen in fact before the Panathenaea, 705 days before the terminus to which interest was reckoned, while 424-3 and 423-2 were both ordinary years in the civil calendar (cf. Chap. IX, Part I, below). This proof may be anticipated here as substantiating the interpretation I have given above, and we may note in passing the bearing it has on our knowledge of the term of office of various boards. Not only did the stewards of sacred moneys hold office from Panathenaea to Panathenaea, but this period was the term of office of the hellenotamiae as well. Keil denied this (*Hermes*, 1894, p. 57), claiming that their term of office was the senatorial year, but Keil's interpretation must be abandoned, partly because he assumed that 424-3 was an intercalated year in the civil calendar (*op. cit.*, p. 58) and partly because he could not know that the payment in question must have been made before the Panathenaic festival. He was forced to take refuge in the assumption that the hellenotamiae mentioned in this inscription received the payment during their term of εὔθυνα, but this assumption raises a question still harder to explain. Why was not the money given to the acting board, rather than to a board which had ceased to function and which was undergoing its final scrutiny? Granting, however, that the hellenotamiae held office from Panathenaea to Panathenaea, the interpretation which I have outlined above allows the following sequence of events. The money was actually paid before the Panathenaea; it was recorded as the first item of state expenditure in the senatorial year 424-3, which also began before the Panathenaea; and the hellenotamiae who received the money, and who also left office at the time of the Panathenaea, were referred to naturally as the board of the previous year.

On the basis of the preceding argument I restore *I.G.* I², 324, lines 27-28 as [- - - ἐπὶ τῆς ἱπποθοντίδος πρυτανείας πρότες πρυτανε]υόσες ἥκτει καὶ εἰκοστῆι τῆς πρυτανεί[ας - - -].

We may now return to a consideration of how our conclusions drawn so far affect Keil's reasoning as to the correspondences between the civil and the senatorial years. Keil assumes that the senatorial years from 426-5 to 423-2 contained 1440 days (360 days each). We now know that these four senatorial years contained 1464 days, and Keil's scheme must in consequence be discarded. We shall return later to a constructive study of the calendar during the latter part of the fifth century, but we may note at present merely that the regular succession of senatorial years, each containing 360 or 390 days, which Keil thought to have been instituted at the time of Kleisthenes, and upon which he builds his calendar system, is a demonstrated impossibility. This is a somewhat disconcerting discovery, especially when one realizes how many of the dates in Greek history have been accepted on the basis of Keil's tables, but we have no alternative other than to admit that his hypothesis is not borne out in fact.

The three large fragments of our inscription, *a*, *b*, and *f*, had been set into a bed of plaster in the museum in Athens, and through the courtesy of Mr. Leonardos,

the Director of the Epigraphical Museum, I was permitted to remove enough of the
plaster between the fragments to test the smaller pieces for possible joins. Fragment *d*

Photograph IV. Frg. *d*.

(See Photograph IV) actually joins the upper edge of frg. *f* in the position indicated
in Plate I, and the text is determined as follows:

62   – – – – – τόκ]ος τού[το – – – – – – – – – – – – –

            – – – – –]γσι ΤΧΧΧΧ ΙϜ[– – – – – – – – –

            – – – – – – ·]ΗΗΔΔΠϜΙ τόκο[ς τούτο – – – – –

65   – – – – – –]ΔϜϜϜϜΙΙΙΙ τόκο[ς τούτο – – – – –

            – – – – – –]ϜϜϜΙΙΙΙΙC *v* Μοσ[õν – – – – – –

            – – 'Αδρασ]τείας ⊡ΔΔΔΠϜ τό[κος τούτο – – – –

            – – – – –]ΙC) *v* 'Απόλλον[ος – – – – – – – –

            – – – – – –]ηερακλέος ἐν [Κυνοσάργει   – – – –

70   – – – Δεμ]οφõντος [. . .⁶. . .] τόκος τούτ[ο – – –

71   τόκο]ς τούτο ΗΔΔΠϜϜϜϜΙΙΙC) *v* 'Απόλλο[νος – –

In line 63 the first three letters are clearly *gamma, sigma,* and *iota,* a combination which is meaningless and permits of no restoration, though an explanation of these letters is offered below. In the same line the last numerical sign cannot have represented 100 Dr., for enough of the stone is preserved to show that the right vertical bar did not exist. The figure was Ⱶ, and before it is the short vertical bar of Π. But it is impossible to say whether the figure should be restored as ⊞, ⊡, or Π.

In line 66 the numeral should be read − −]ⱵⱵⱵΙΙΙΙⅭ, as by Kirchhoff. In line 69 the left vertical bar of the *nu* is on the stone and before it the *epsilon* is perfectly preserved. The final *nu* of line 71 is now lost.

The placing of frg. *d* makes possible the placing also of frg. *k* (See Photograph V) and the determination of the relative positions of the upper and lower sections of the inscription. This determination is effected by studying the names of

Photograph V. Frg. *k.*

the various divinities whose money is recorded in the payments of the Other Gods, and by the observation that in the record of both payments the order of the names of these divinities is the same. For the position of the fragments *cf.* Plate I, and for the text *cf.* the accompanying transcript, Plate II.

I give here a table of correspondences between the names from these two payments to show the identity of the order. The numbering of the lines throughout follows the transcript.

Payment I		Payment II	
Artemis Agrotera	59	Artemis Agrotera	79
[Aphrodite in the Gardens]	59	Aphrodite in the Gardens	80
Unknown	60	Unknown	81
[Dionysus]	61	Dionysus	8,1
Unknown	61	Unknown	82
Poseidon at Sunium	62	Poseidon at Sunium	82
Unknown	63	Unknown	83
Artemis Munichia	63	Artemis Munichia	83
[Theseus]	64	Theseus	84
[Ilissus]	64	Ilissus	84
Unknown	65	Unknown	85
[Hephaestus]	65	Hephaestus	85
Aphrodite by Hippolyteion	66	Aphrodite by Hippolyteion	85-86
Muses	66	Muses	86
	—	Foreign God	86
Apollo at Zoster	67		—
Adrasteia	67		—
Bendis (?)	68		—
Unknown	68		—
Apollo	68		—
Unknown	69		—
Herakles in Kynosarges	69	Herakles in Kynosarges	87
He (?)	70		—
Demophon	70	Demophon	87
Athena in Pallenis	71	Athena in Pallenis	88
Apollo	71	Apollo	88
Artemis Bauronia	72	Artemis Brauronia	89
Unknown	73	Unknown	90
Athena by the Palladium	73	Athena by the Palladium	90
Unknown	74	Unknown	91
Poseidon Kalaureates	74		—
	—	Mother in Agrae	91
	—	Unknown	92
	—	Athena at Zoster	92
	—	Unknown	93

Fragment *k* may be assigned to the left margin of the inscription because of the characteristic bevelled edge which it displays, and the order of the names preserved on the fragment determines its definite position along that margin. In particular, notice that the words Ἀφροδίτες ἐν ἱππολυ[τείοι from frg. *k* immediately precede and fall on the same line with Μοσ[ὸν from frg. *d*. Also the word Δεμ]οφõντος from frg. *f* immediately precedes and falls at the end of the line just above Ἀθενα]ί[ας ἐπὶ] Παλλ[ενίδι from frg. *k*.

This last line of frg. *k* is not given in the transcript in the *Corpus*, but the significant letters may be seen in Photograph V. I have restored the words ἐπὶ] Παλλ[ενίδι instead of ἐν] Παλλ[ενίδι because the longer form is required by the *stoichedon* arrangement of letters in the inscription. In the text of the *Corpus* the item Ἀθε[ναίας ἐν Παλλ]ενίδι is given in the record of the second payment from the treasure of the Other Gods (line 93), but here also the *stoichedon* arrangement of the letters demands the longer restoration. I suggest Ἀθε[ναίας ἐπὶ Παλλ]ενίδι, and this form appears in the transcript (Plate II, line 88). For the order of the letters, see Plate I.

In the first line of frg. *k* the suggested restoration τόκος τούτ]ο is impossible, because if the numeral here is classified as a sum of interest, it raises the sum total of the individual amounts of interest to a figure higher than that preserved for the sum total in line 76. The figure here represents principal and the word to be restored before it must be the name of the divinity to whom the money belonged.

The relation of the lower group of fragments in this inscription to the upper group may now be determined on the basis of the order in which the names of the divinities appear in the two payments made from the treasure of the Other Gods. It may be seen from the above table that the names from *Artemis Agrotera* to the *Muses* run exactly parallel in the records of both payments. With due consideration for the amount of space which each item occupies within the line, it appears that the words Ποσειδõνος ἐπὶ Σουνίοι of frg. *n* (belonging to the upper group of fragments) fall four lines above Ἀφροδίτες ἐν ἱππολυτείοι of frg. *k* (belonging to the lower group of fragments). At the same time we discover that the enigmatic letters in the second line of frg. *d* must be interpreted as part of the item [Ἀρτέμιδος Μονιχί]ας and that this line falls immediately below Ποσειδõνος ἐπὶ Σουνίοι in frg. *n* above. When the fragments are so placed the order of names is the same in both payments and we find also a possible explanation for the letters ΛΣΙ which appear at the beginning of the second line of frg. *d*.

Of these three letters the *gamma* was clearly meant for an *alpha*, but the cross-bar was omitted by the stonecutter. The *sigma* is correct as it stands, and these two letters form the end of the word Μουνιχί]ας. Following the *sigma*, however, there is still an *iota* unexplained, for it cannot belong to the word Μουνιχίας. I assume that here too the stonecutter neglected to add the horizontal bar at the top of the letter and that the *iota* must be read as an incomplete *tau*. It is, in fact, part of the numeral which gives the amount of money drawn from the treasure of Artemis Munichia, and we may now restore this numeral as (T)TXXXXΓҤ− − − (See above, p. 21).

There are two other minor matters of text determination which may be noted here. The numeral, for example, in the first line of frg. *k* (line 65 of the transcript) is clearly XΓHHHHⱣΔΔΓҤII[− − − . There is a possibility that some obols have been lost from the end. Also, we have shown in our table above that the name of Aphrodite by the Hippolyteion precedes the name of the Muses in both payments from the treasure of the Other Gods, and we give in our transcript the restoration Ἀφ[ροδίτες ἐν hιπ
πολυτείοι] (lines 85-86) where the *Corpus* text reads Ἀθ[εναίας− −]. As a matter of fact the disputed letter is actually a *phi*, with the left rounding and the lower tip of the vertical bar preserved on the stone. This is indicated in Plate I.

Photograph VI. Frg. *p*.

There is still one small fragment, *p*, which must be discussed in its relation to the rest of the inscription.

(See Photograph VI)

− − − − − − −]XHΔ[− − −

− − − τόκος το]ύτο ΔҤ[−

− − − τόκο]ς τούτο [− − −

− − − Γοργ]οίνο [ἀρχ − − − −

− − − − − −]ερ[− − − − − −

This piece also has the characteristic bevelled edge on the left, and so comes from the left side of the stone. The key to its position is given, I think, by the letters of the fourth line, which should be restored to give the name of the chief treasurer Gorgoinus. And we find the appropriate place for this fragment at the beginning of lines 73-77 (*cf.* Plates I and II).

Notice also, in Plate I, that a line of breakage runs diagonally up from left to right along the edge of fragments *p*, *k*, and *n*. This line of breakage is continuous with the fragments placed as determined above and as indicated in our plate, and offers an additional proof that the proposed reconstruction is correct.

But we have not spoken as yet about one of the major problems of reconstructing the stele. Along both sides of the stone the edge has been bevelled back by some post-Classical mason. That this bevelled edge does not represent the original margin of the stone is at once apparent to anyone who attempts the restoration of the document; and in fact the line of cutting on both sides runs directly through some of the letters along the margin, so that they are at present only partially preserved on the stone. The angle at which this bevelled edge was made is approximately the same on both sides and it is a reasonable *a priori* assumption that about the same number of letters have been lost from each line beyond the right and left margins of the stone as it is preserved today. This fact has been recognized by the editors of the *Corpus* in their publication of fragment *f,* and the present edge of the stone, which dates from post-Classical times, has been given in its proper relation to the original edge of the stone.

In the publication of frgs. *a, b,* and *c,* however, (the upper section of the stone) the post-Classical edge has been identified with the original edge along the right margin, while along the left margin ten letters have been restored instead of four in each line, to the left of the similar post-Classical edge. This is obviously an incorrect arrangement, for the post-Classical edge should be made to run continuously from the upper to the lower section of the stele, as represented in our facsimile (Plate I), and part of the ten letters now restored at the beginning of the lines in the upper section of the document must be transferred to the ends of the lines in order to preserve the symmetry of the stone.

This change affects the readings in the initial line of the inscription, and also in other lines which begin new rubrics at the left margin of the stele. For example, we must read in line 1: τάδε ἐλογίσαντο hοι λογισταὶ etc., instead of τάδε τε͂ς θεο͂ ἐλογίσαντο hοι λογισταὶ etc. And in line 54 we must read τάδε ἐλογίσαντο hοι λογισταὶ etc., instead of τάδε το͂ τόκο ἐλογίσαντο hοι λογισταὶ etc. It appears that the heading in line 1 was general in its application and referred to the audit of all the accounts mentioned in the inscription, not merely to those of Athena.

We have been able, fortunately, to assign to every fragment its definite place in the inscription, and we give in Plate I what we believe to be the correct disposition. The fragments themselves, so far as preserved, have also been so arranged in a bed of plaster in the Epigraphical Museum at Athens.

We now have before us the reconstructed document and it is our problem to build up the text by careful restoration. Much may depend on even a single letter, and I have consequently made a careful revision of the stones. Some comment should be appended here on the readings shown in Plate I, for on that the transcript in Plate II is based.

Line 6: The numeral has been restored correctly by Keil, and I agree with him that no alternative is possible (*cf. Hermes,* 1894, p. 62). There seems to be on the stone the mere corner of a second Δ. Toward the end of line 6 the reading λοι[παί is certain. I have chosen to restore the number of days as ηεπτά instead of πέντε as in the *Corpus,* for reasons which will appear below. The restorations are equally possible epigraphically.

Line 9: The interest on the third payment is ΤΧ⌐ΗΗΔ⌐ΗΗΗΗΙΙ, or at least this is the number cut on the stone, and it may be distinguished today in its entirety. The reading of this numeral has been correctly given by Rangabé, *Ant. Hell.,* no. 116.

Line 10: The word ἐμέρας is clear on the stone, and the word following it must be restored as ἐσελελυθυίας, in spite of the violation of the *stoichedon* order of the letters. Pittakys, no. 2266, gives this correctly.

Line 14: The amount of interest actually preserved on the stone is ΧΧΧΧΗ⌐ΔΔΗΗΙ[– – . These numerals are perfectly clear, and are given in the transcripts of Velsen, Ross, Pittakys, and Rangabé. I do not know why the figures ΧΧΧΧ have been omitted from both editions of the *Corpus.*

Line 15: The sum total of the payments for the first year is given on the stone as ΗΗΗ⌐ΔΤ⌐ΗΗΗ[– . It is a simple mathematical problem in maxima and minima to demonstrate that the numeral given in the *Corpus* should be restored as indicated above in any case, but since the numbers are actually on the stone, the mathematical demonstration is not necessary.

Line 17: Note the fact that one letter space is left uninscribed at the end of this line.

Lines 18-19: The name of the prytanizing tribe must be restored either as Οἰνεῖδος or as Αἰγεῖδος. I have chosen Αἰγεῖδος because of the probable connection between this passage and *I.G.* I², 63, lines 33-35. This connection is interesting also as giving the date when the discussion was opened in the assembly on Cleon's proposal to double the tribute—the third day of the fourth prytany in the year 425-4 (*cf.* Chap. IX, Part I).

Line 26: The name of the first secretary of the senate in the year 424-3 has been restored as ['Επί]λ[υ]κος. Cf. P. Haggard, The Secretaries of the Athenian Boule in the Fifth Century, *Transactions and Proceedings of the American Philological Association,* LVII, 1926, pp. xxxi-xxxii. Miss Haggard reads ['Επί]λυκος.

Line 32: The numeral given in the *Corpus* at the beginning of this line as

a doubtful Ḥ (100 Dr.) is preceded by a vertical stroke which may represent a
second 100 drachmae sign. The left margin of the fragment is so broken, however,
at this point that all trace of the central bar of the H is missing; and even in the case
of the numeral given in the *Corpus* a pot-mark caused by erosion has eaten away the
face of the marble, so that the lower portions of the upright strokes are no longer
preserved (except for the extreme tip of the left vertical bar). The surface of the stone
where the cross-bar of the H once existed has been completely destroyed by erosion.
So far as one may judge from surface indications the strokes preserved may represent
3 obols, rather than 200 Dr., and it would be necessary to admit the possibility of
either interpretation if it were not for the fact that the erosion has preserved the form
of the H, in spite of the fact that the surface is gone.[1] At many points on the stone
the surface has suffered from the corrosive effects of the elements, and yet it may be
generally observed that the corrosion has proceeded more rapidly along the lines cut
by the mason's chisel. In places where the letter *omicron,* for example, has been
completely eaten away so that none of the surface is preserved, there still remains the
circular ring, corroded more deeply than the small island of uninscribed stone which
it enclosed, in such a way that we may be certain that the letter was *omicron.* The
same process was active in the case of the numeral now under discussion, and
although the original surface which contained the chiselled marks of the cross-bar
and lower vertical strokes of the H has been weathered away, the corroded surface
which we see today exhibits clearly the deeper depressions where these strokes made
the marble more susceptible to the action of the weather. We may see also the
relatively less corroded surface where the original uninscribed portion offered greater
resistance. The figure may be read without hesitation as H, and the numeral to be
restored at the beginning of line 32 ended in symbols representing 200 Dr.

Line 37: The *rho* of ἐγραμμάτευε is partially preserved on the stone, as given
by Pittakys, no. 2267.

Line 39: An *iota* is preserved on the stone before the initial *tau* given in
the *Corpus.*

Line 41: The numeral preserved on the stone reads HℙΔⱵⱵⱵIIII[— — as given
by Pittakys, no. 2267.

Line 42: Before the initial *tau* given in this line in the *Corpus,* Ross read an
initial *rho* (*cf.* Boeckh, *Kleine Schriften,* Vol. VI, p. 90). Boeckh proposed to read *kappa*
instead of *rho.* I have examined the stone and am convinced that the letter may be

---

[1] Doubt as to the reading is expressed by Bratuscheck and Eichholtz in Boeckh's *Kleine Schriften,*
Vol. VI, p. 90, and note.

either *rho* or *pi,* but not *kappa.* The letter *rho* seems more probable, as shown in Plate I.

Line 72: Velsen's notes give a horizontal stroke as though it belonged to a second *delta* at the end of this line. The stone is broken away, however, and there is now preserved only so much as was seen, apparently, by Pittakys (no. 1204 δίς, p. 830), giving a portion of one *delta* at the end of the line.

Line 74: Before the preserved numeral H in the first line of frg. *e* there is a stroke which can be interpreted only as part of the figure 𐅅, as represented in Plate I. For the shape of the numeral, see the figure 𐅅 at the beginning of line 51.

Line 79: Comment has been made above (pp. 9-11) on the reading of this line.

Line 80: Before the numerals of frg. *e* in this line the stone is so preserved as to make certain that no numeral preceded the initial *delta* now on the stone. The words τόκος τούτο may, in consequence, be restored.

Line 84: The initial numerals of this line are clearly – –]⊢̣ΙΙ as shown in Plate I. In this line also the amount of principal borrowed from Ilissus must be restored as HHHH⊢⊢̣Ι. The spacing of the numerals shows that the next to the last figure must have represented a drachma.

Line 85: We have already noticed that the last letter of this line is *phi,* not *theta,* as previously given (*cf.* p. 24 above).

Line 86: The initial numerals in frg. *e* are clearly ⊢ΙΙ, not ΙΙΙΙ as represented in the *Corpus.* It has already been noticed that the payment made from the treasure of the Muses is wrongly given as 𐅄ΔΔ⊢. The figures are 𐅅ΔΔ⊢.

Line 114: The last three numerals of the sum total of payments made by Athena Polias are on the stone today, as they were recorded by Pittakys, Velsen, and Rangabé. *Cf.* Plate I.

Line 115: This numeral is preserved in its entirety on the stone, but after the figures -𐅅HH only the tops of the remaining figures are left. These are so spaced (*cf.* Plate I) that the numeral must be restored ҲHHΔΔΔTTTXXX𐅅HHH⊢⊢⊢. The break in the surface of the stone seems to follow, in fact, the horizontal bars of the last three drachma signs. Portions of the cutting for the last two of these are still visible.

The inscription as a whole is written with a *stoichedon* arrangement of the letters which is followed with rare exception in the upper part of the document. We have already seen that the order was violated once in line 10, where the word ἐσελελυθυίας was written in the space normally allowed for eleven letters. We shall see later that the name of the prytanizing tribe in line 51 contained only ten letters, although it occupied eleven letter spaces on the stone. Large numerals such as 𐅅 and

ᚺ were apt to occupy more than one space. For example, the four figures ᚺᚺ𐅅Δ in line 15 occupied five letter spaces, and the numeral 𐅄 in line 49 occupied two letter spaces. In this upper part of the inscription, down to line 37, with the exception of lines 10 and 17, there were 75 letter spaces in each line. From line 38 to line 75 the number of letter spaces in a line varies from 74 to 75, and below line 75 there were never more than 74 letter spaces, though sometimes less, in each line. In this lower part of the inscription, especially from line 94 on, the *stoichedon* order of letters and numerals, especially numerals, is often neglected.

CHAPTER III

METHODS OF RECKONING INTEREST

For a study of the problems of restoration which involve mathematical computation a most convenient point of departure is found in the record of payments from the money of Athena Polias in the year 426-5. Here the six individual items of interest must be added together in such a way that they give the sum total of interest for this year as it is recorded in line 16.

Interest on Payment I	[ⵀⵔHⵟΔΔ]ΔΔⵔⵑ	*cf.* p. 26 above
Interest on Payment II	ⵜⵜXⵔHHHHⵟΔΔ	
Iuterest on Payment III	ⵜXⵔHHΔⵔⵑⵑⵑⵑII	
Interest on Payment IV	?	
Interest on Payment V	ⵜⵜⵜⵀⵔHHHHΔΔΔ	
Interest on Payment VI	XXXXHⵟΔΔⵑⵑI[− −	
Total interest	[. ³ .]ⵟΔΔΔΔⵔⵑⵑⵑI	

Fortunately the significant figures of the total interest are preserved, and it is possible to determine within a few obols what the fourth amount of interest must have been. We are helped also by the knowledge that the fourth payment was made on the fifth day of the eighth prytany, and it is possible to tell within very narrow limits the number of days for which the payment was outstanding. The fifth payment was made on either the 6th, 8th, or 10th day of the eighth prytany (the numeral of date to be restored contains four letters, either hέχς, ὀκτό, or δέκα) and we know that this payment was outstanding 1197 days. Inasmuch as the fourth payment was made on the fifth day of the same prytany, it must have been outstanding either 1198, 1200, or 1202 days, depending on whether we restore hέχς, ὀκτό, or δέκα in line 11.

Furthermore we know that the principal of the fourth payment was either $44\frac{1}{2}$ or $48\frac{1}{2}$ talents, for the only restorations possible for this amount in line 10 are ΔΔΔΔ[T]TTTXXX and ΔΔΔΔ[Π]TTTXXX. It is a simple matter to compute the six sums of interest thus made possible by the two different amounts of principal and the three different periods of time, for interest throughout this inscription was reckoned at the rate: 5 talents in one day yields one drachma. Calculated by our modern decimal system of computation the results are as follows:

1. $44\frac{1}{2}$ talents in 1198 days yields 10662.2 Dr.   TXXXXΓHΓΔⱵⱵIC
2. $44\frac{1}{2}$ talents in 1200 days yields 10680   Dr.   TXXXXΓHΓΔΔΔ
3. $44\frac{1}{2}$ talents in 1202 days yields 10697.8 Dr.   TXXXXΓHΓΔΔΔΔΠⱵⱵIIIC
4. $48\frac{1}{2}$ talents in 1198 days yields 11620.6 Dr.   TⲘΓHΔΔIIII
5. $48\frac{1}{2}$ talents in 1200 days yields 11640   Dr.   TⲘΓHΔΔΔ
6. $48\frac{1}{2}$ talents in 1202 days yields 11659.4 Dr.   TⲘΓHΓΠⱵⱵⱵIII

These figures are all mathematically sound, and some one of them should give, when added to the other five amounts listed above, the required sum total. It is a disturbing fact that this is not the case, but of one thing we may be certain, that the amounts of interest reckoned on $48\frac{1}{2}$ talents give a total amount of interest so far divergent from that preserved on the stone as to be surely wrong. The amount of principal to be restored in line 10 must be ΔΔΔΔ[T]TTTXXX, and this numeral is in fact that which Pittakys read in its entirety on the stone (Pittakys no. 2267), though it is possible that Pittakys restored the missing numeral without indicating his restoration. Even with this principal the interest accrued for 1198 days or 1200 days gives a total so much at variance with that on the stone as to be surely wrong.

Only with the interest on $44\frac{1}{2}$ talents for 1202 days do we approach the correct solution, and here the sum total of the individual amounts of interest adds to [ΔTH]ΓΔΔΔΔΠⱵ etc., with a discrepancy of almost four drachmae from the numeral which we may restore on the stone: [ΔTH]ΓΔΔΔΔΠⱵⱵⱵI.

I presume that others have arrived at this same *impasse* in trying to restore the inscription, and I have more than once been inclined to agree with Keil's remark «Ich halte die Versuche, die Zahlen der Inschrift namentlich in den Jahren 2-4 wiederherstellen zu wollen, für absolut aussichtslos – – – durch langwierige Berechnungen hatte ich den Standpunkt der Resignation gewonnen». But the problem here at least ought not to be so difficult. We have an answer which differs from the correct answer by about four drachmae. It is impossible to rectify this by modifying the interest on the first payment, or by changing the restoration of the final possible obol signs in the interest on the sixth payment, for the significant figures are all on the stone. The amounts of interest on payments II, III, and V are preserved in their entirety and no change is possible. In fact, we are apparently left with one of two possible assumptions. Either:

(a) the auditors reckoned the amount of interest correctly on payment IV, but made some mistake in addition, so that the total differs from the one we have obtained, or

(b) the auditors made some small error in computing the interest on the fourth payment, or perhaps on the third or sixth payments.

This seems to be the dilemma, but I think we need not charge the official board of audit with error in this instance. We shall find proof later that they did sometimes make mistakes, but in this case another explanation is possible.

Our amount of interest on the fourth payment was computed by the use of decimal notation, which is an exact mathematical implement not at the disposal of the ancient Greeks. They certainly used some other system of computation and they may well have obtained a result different from ours, and yet correct when judged in the light of the method they used. We know, for example, that fractions were a standing difficulty, and that approximations were often used. An almost infinitessimal margin of error in the reckoning of one day's interest might easily amount to four or five drachmae when multiplied by 1202, which is the number of days for which this payment was outstanding. We can foresee some of the difficulties which must have troubled the board of auditors when we realize that the rate of interest was $\frac{1}{5}$ Dr. per day per talent, and when we realize further that the talent and the drachma found their natural divisions in *sixths,* and that the obol was divided by *halves* and *quarters.*

With this in mind I have drawn up the following table which may be used in reference, and which gives the correspondence between principal and interest for one day, with the interest expressed in multiples of $\frac{1}{4}$ obol.[1]

	1250 Dr.	yields	in	one	day		⟩
	2500 Dr.	»	»	»	»		⊂
	3750 Dr.	»	»	»	»		⊂⟩
	5000 Dr.	»	»	»	»			
1 Tal.	250 Dr.	»	»	»	»		|⟩
1 Tal.	1500 Dr.	»	»	»	»		|⊂

---

[1] I am very much indebted to Mr. Jotham Johnson, Fellow of the American School of Classical Studies, for suggesting this table to me, and for his assistance in demonstrating the practical advantages of its use in the restoration of this inscription.

1 Tal.	2750 Dr.	yields	in	one	day	IC⟩
1 Tal.	4000 Dr.	»	»	»	»	II
1 Tal.	5250 Dr.	»	»	»	»	II⟩
2 Tal.	500 Dr.	»	»	»	»	IIC
2 Tal.	1750 Dr.	»	»	»	»	IIC⟩
2 Tal.	3000 Dr.	»	»	»	»	III
2 Tal.	4250 Dr.	»	»	»	»	III⟩
2 Tal.	5500 Dr.	»	»	»	»	IIIC
3 Tal.	750 Dr.	»	»	»	»	IIIC⟩
3 Tal.	2000 Dr.	»	»	»	»	IIII
3 Tal.	3250 Dr.	»	»	»	»	IIII⟩
3 Tal.	4500 Dr.	»	»	»	»	IIIIC
3 Tal.	5750 Dr.	»	»	»	»	IIIIC⟩
4 Tal.	1000 Dr.	»	»	»	»	IIIII
4 Tal.	2250 Dr.	»	»	»	»	IIIII⟩
4 Tal.	3500 Dr.	»	»	»	»	IIIIIC
4 Tal.	4750 Dr.	»	»	»	»	IIIIIC⟩
5 Talents		»	»	»	»	Ͱ

There is no need to carry the table farther than 5 talents in the column of amounts of principal, for there was no difficulty in reckoning interest on 5 talents or on any multiple of 5 talents. It is possible that the accounts with which we are dealing were reckoned according to this table, with fractional amounts which did not agree with the key figures in the column of amounts of principal handled by approximation. We do not know the kind of abacus which the auditors used to assist them in their reckoning, but the fractions $\frac{1}{2}$ and $\frac{1}{3}$ were certainly amenable to their processes of computation, as were the fractions derived from these two by multiplication, like $\frac{1}{4}, \frac{1}{6}, \frac{1}{8}, \frac{1}{9}, \frac{1}{12}, \frac{1}{16}$, etc. Fifths and tenths were avoided, as were also the odd fractions $\frac{1}{7}, \frac{1}{11}, \frac{1}{13}, \frac{1}{14}, \frac{1}{15}, \frac{1}{17}$, etc.

Or it is possible that interest was reckoned on an amount of principal by considering in turn the various figures which were the component parts of the sum. For example, to reckon interest on ΔΔΔΔΤΤΤΤΧΧΧ for 1202 days, the auditors might first consider the 40 talents, then the 4 talents, and then the 3000 drachmae, if in fact they did not consider each separate figure individually. This scheme of reckoning will appear as a possibility when we recall how the Greeks themselves thought about a large numerical amount. Evidence for this is at hand in this inscription, in those lines where the sums total of principal accrued during the seven years from 433 to 426 are recorded.

In lines 98-100, instead of writing out the amount of principal reckoned by the previous boards of auditors in numerical signs as ✗✗✗✗TXXXX𐅆ΔΔ⊦⊦, the amount is expressed in words: τετρακισχιλίοις ταλάντοις ταλάντοι τετρακισχιλίαις πεντακοσίαις εἴκοσι δυοῖν δραχμαῖν. And again in lines 103-105, instead of writing out in numerical signs the accumulated principal owing to the Other Gods as 𐅇ΗΗ𐅇Δ𐅆ΤΧ𐅆ΔΔΔΔ𐅂ΙΙΙΙΙ, the amount is expressed in words: πεντακοσίοις ταλάντοις διακοσίοις ταλάντοις ἑχσέχοντα ταλάντοις ἑχς ταλάντοις χιλίαις ἐνενέχοντα δραχμαῖς πέντε δραχμαῖς πέντε ὀβολοῖς. In lines 107-108 instead of writing in numerical signs the principal due to Athena Nike from the previous seven year period as ΔΔΤΤΧΧΧ𐅆ΔΔΔΔ𐅂⊦⊦ΙΙ, the amount is expressed in words: εἴκοσι ταλάντοις δυοῖν ταλάντοιν τρισχιλίαις ἐνενέχοντα δραχμαῖς ὀκτὸ δραχμαῖς δυοῖν ὀβολοῖν.

Particularly in the second example cited above it is clear that the whole amount was thought of in terms of its component parts, i.e., 𐅇ΗΗ𐅇Δ𐅆ΤΧ𐅆ΔΔΔΔ𐅂ΙΙΙΙΙ was construed as the sum of the following amounts:

1. 𐅇
2. ΗΗ
3. 𐅇Δ
4. 𐅆Τ
5. Χ𐅆ΔΔΔΔ
6. 𐅂
7. ΙΙΙΙΙ

With this in mind I have drawn up also the following table which may be used in the computing of interest on amounts expressed by one numerical symbol.

𐅆	in one day yields	⊦
Τ	in 5 days yields	⊦
𐅇	in one day yields	Ι
Χ	in 5 days yields	Ι
𐅆	in 5 days yields	Ϲ
Η	in 25 days yields	Ϲ
𐅇	in 25 days yields	)
Δ	in 125 days yields	)
𐅂	in 250 days yields	)
⊦	in 1250 days yields	)

Again there is the possibility of a margin of error because fractions develop whenever the number of days for which the payment was outstanding is not exactly divisible by 5, or 25, or 125, etc., as the case may be. These fractions may have been reckoned as whole numbers, neglected, or approximated, and in any case the result obtained is apt to vary from that which we should obtain today by the use of the decimal system.

We do not know of course, *a priori,* which one of these methods was used, or whether it may have been a combination of both, but the justification for the first table proposed above is that it brings us out of the dilemma which we encountered in trying to make the six separate items of interest in the year 426-5 add to equal the sum total of the interest as that number is preserved on the stone.

By this first method we may reckon the interest on 44 $\frac{1}{2}$ talents for 1202 days as follows:

40 Tal.		in	one	day	yields	8 Dr.	
4 Tal.	2250 Dr.	in	one	day	yields		5 $\frac{1}{4}$ obols
	750 Dr.	in	one	day	yields		

$\frac{3}{5} \times \frac{1}{4}$ obols, which may be approximated to $\frac{4}{6} \times \frac{1}{4}$ obols $= \frac{1}{6}$ obol $\quad = \quad \frac{1}{6}$ obol

44 Tal.	3000 Dr.	in	one	day	yields	8 Dr. 5 $\frac{5}{12}$ obols
44 Tal.	3000 Dr.	in	1202	days	yields	10701 Dr. 1 obol.

If we now restore this numeral as the interest on the fourth payment we find that it fills exactly the space required on the stone at the end of line 10 (TXXXXΓHHHΗΙ) leaving the usual uninscribed space of one letter before and after the numeral, and if we restore the interest on the sixth payment as XXXXHΓΔΔΗΗΙ[III] we discover also that the six sums of interest may be added to give the total as it appears on the stone.

Interest on Payment	I		5696 Dr.	
Interest on Payment	II	2 Tal.	1970 Dr.	
Interest on Payment	III	1 Tal.	1719 Dr.	2 obols
Interest on Payment	IV	1 Tal.	4701 Dr.	1 obol
Interest on Payment	V	3 Tal.	5940 Dr.	
Interest on Payment	VI		4172 Dr.	4 obols
Total Sum of Interest		11 Tal.	199 Dr.	1 obol.

This sum total, when written in Greek numerical characters, is ΔTHΓΔΔΔΔΠΗΗΗΙ, and this numeral should be restored in line 16.

Incidentally we learn that the number of days to be restored at the end of line 11 is δέκα, and that the fourth payment was outstanding 1202 days. Our previous conclusion, that the amount of principal to be restored as the fourth payment is ΔΔΔΔ[Τ]ΤΤΤΧΧΧ is confirmed.

Sometimes the approximation reached by the use of this first table was corrected, possibly by the use of the second table. We find, for example, in lines 103-105 that the amount of principal borrowed from the treasurers of the Other Gods and totaling 766 talents, 1095 drachmae, and 5 obols was outstanding throughout the whole four year period of 1464 days. By table I the interest on this amount is reckoned as follows:

765 Tal.		in one day yields 153 Dr.		
		in 1464 days yields		223992 Dr.
1 Tal.	250 Dr.	in one day yields $1\frac{1}{4}$ obols		
		in 1464 days yields 1830 obols	=	305 Dr.
	845 Dr.	5 obols yields in one day $\frac{846}{1250}$ (app.) $\times \frac{1}{4}$ obol $= \frac{1}{6}$ obol		
		in 1464 days yields 244 obols	=	40 Dr. 4 obols

766 Tal. 1095 Dr. 5 obols in 1464 days yields   224337 Dr. 4 obols

To obtain this result, however, we approximated the fraction $\frac{846}{1250}$ to $\frac{2}{3}$, whereas in reality $\frac{833\,1/3}{1250} = \frac{2}{3}$. In other words we have not as yet reckoned the interest on $12\frac{2}{3}$ Dr. for the period of 1464 days. If this correction is made by the second table above the amount of interest obtained is within one obol of that preserved on the stone.

Or perhaps the total sum was reckoned on the basis of the next higher key figure in the first table, as follows:

765 Tal.		in one day yields 153 Dr.		
		in 1464 days yields	223992 Dr.	
1 Tal.	1500 Dr.	in one day yields $1\frac{1}{2}$ obols		
		in 1464 days yields 2196 obols	=	366 Dr.

766 Tal. 1500 Dr. in 1464 days yields   224358 Dr.

Here however we have reckoned on a sum too high by 1500-1096 = 404 Dr. We may make the correction by the second table again, reckoning interest on each 101 Dr. as $29\frac{1}{2}$ obols. Interest on 404 Dr. then amounts to 118 obols = $19\frac{4}{6}$ Dr., which sum may be subtracted from 224358 Dr. to give a sum only $\frac{1}{2}$ obol less than the figure preserved on the stone. The same result is obtained by the use of the decimal system in computing the interest.

We thus see that no one of these systems of reckoning gives exactly the result found on the stone, probably because of some difference in the approximation of the odd fraction. When the amount of the principal is exactly divisible by five talents there is of course no difficulty in the calculation of interest. When the fractional remainder after the amount has been divided by five talents corresponds with one of the key figures in the first table above, there is no element of uncertainty. But if the fractional remainder does not in any given case coincide with one of the key amounts in the first table above, the necessity of approximation may arise, with its attendant element of error. Accuracy, as we understand the term today, was not in every instance attainable, and we must remember, in studying the amounts of interest preserved in the inscription, that a slight variation is possible from the amount as it would now be obtained by the use of decimal notation.

CHAPTER IV

TOTALS OF PRINCIPAL BORROWED FROM ATHENA POLIAS

We must leave for the time being the attempt to restore the remaining numerals and dates in the record of the year 426-5 and turn to the more complicated problem of the sum total of amounts of principal reckoned during the quadrennium.

We have in line 49 the sum total of moneys borrowed from Athena Polias from 426 to 422. The numeral is not preserved entire, but the beginning of the amount may be restored with certainty by the addition of the figure ⱈ. This restoration has been made in the *Corpus*, and, indeed, is evident from the comparison of this amount with the amount expressed in words in lines 99-100, and the sum total of both these amounts which is preserved in line 114. The end of the numeral in line 49 remains as yet undetermined, and we read

$$[ⱈ]ⱵⱵ\triangle\triangle\triangle\triangleⱈTTX[. . .^6. . .]$$

with the number of spaces lost at the end determined by the position of the numeral on the stone. It is not necessary to assume that all of these spaces were inscribed, although that is possible.

This numeral represents the grand sum total of the individual sums total of the four years from 426 to 422, which we may summarize as follows:

Year I	ⱵⱵⱈ$\triangle$TⱈⱵ[. .³.]	
Year II	Ⱶ[$\triangle\triangle\triangle$]	the restoration is certain. *Cf.* line 23.
Year III	[. . .⁶. . .]	amount unknown, but the number of letter spaces is certain. *Cf.* line 35.
Year IV	[– ²⁻⁴ –]$\triangle\triangle$TTXⱈⱵ$\triangle\triangle\triangle\triangle$ⱵⱵIC	
Total	[ⱈ]ⱵⱵ$\triangle\triangle\triangle\triangle$ⱈTTX[. . .⁶. . .]	

We shall concern ourselves here with the restoration of the amount of the third year, and also the amount of the fourth year, for these two problems must be considered together. Unfortunately we cannot tell at once whether two, three, or four figures should be restored at the beginning of the numeral which represents the total for the fourth year, because the line above may have contained either 74 or 75 letters and there may or may not have been an uninscribed space before the numeral.

But we are able, fortunately, to determine a possible minimum figure for the whole amount, by studying the separate payments made during the fourth year.

1. The first payment was 59 Tal. 4720 Dr. (cf. line 39).

2. The minimum of the second payment was 2 Tal. 5500 Dr. (cf. line 41).

3. For the third payment the amount is not preserved, but the minimum interest is 582 $\frac{1}{6}$ Dr. (cf. line 43). Since this payment may have been made as early as the fourth day of the third prytany,[1] we may determine a maximum number of days for which the payment was outstanding by reckoning back from the last prytany, and assuming a maximum of 40 days in each prytany. We might with safety reckon 39 days as a possible maximum, as will appear later, but it is better here to concede the extra day for purposes of argument. This third payment may have been made, then, $8 \times 40 - 3 = 317$ days before the date to which interest was reckoned.

Now the amount of principal which will yield as interest 582 $\frac{1}{6}$ Dr. in 317 days may be easily determined.

30,000 Dr. (5 Tal.) in 317 days yields 317 Dr.

x Dr.   in 317 days yields 582 $\frac{1}{6}$ Dr.

Algebraically:

$$317 x = 582 \frac{1}{6} \times 30000 = 17465000$$
$$x = 55,094 \text{ Dr.} = 9 \text{ Tal. } 1094 \text{ Dr.}$$

This sum of 9 Tal. 1094 Dr. represents the minimum possible amount of the third payment in the year 423-2.

4. The amount of the fourth payment was 100 talents. (cf. line 44).

5. The amount of the fifth payment is also lost from the stone, but the minimum interest is preserved as 122 $\frac{5}{12}$ Dr. By a process of reckoning similar to that employed in the case of the third payment, we may assume that this payment was made as early as the first day of the last prytany, or 40 days before the terminus to which interest was reckoned, and it may be demonstrated that the minimum possible amount of the principal was 15 Tal. 1812 Dr.

---

[1] For the sake of safety in argument we may disregard for the time being the *rho* or *pi* at the beginning of the preserved portion of line 42 and consider [τρί]τες a possible restoration, as well as [τετά]ρτες or [πέμ]πτες.

These five minimum payments may now be added to give the minimum sum total, as follows:

Payment I	59 Tal.	4720 Dr.
Payment II	2 Tal.	5500 Dr.
Payment III	9 Tal.	1094 Dr.
Payment IV	100 Tal.	
Payment V	15 Tal.	1812 Dr.
Minimum Total	187 Tal.	1126 Dr.

It is, of course, impossible to restore this amount on the stone, the two nearest possibilities being 182 Tal. 1642 $\frac{5}{12}$ Dr. and 192 Tal. 1642 $\frac{5}{12}$ Dr. Of these two figures the former falls below the minimum determined and must be rejected. We may be certain that the latter is the minimum possible restoration, written in Greek numerical characters as follows:

[ΗΓΔΔ]ΔΔΤΤΧΓΗΔΔΔΔΗΗΙΙC.

The next higher amount for this total which is epigraphically possible is 222 Tal. 1642 $\frac{5}{12}$ Dr., to be written in Greek numerical characters as follows:

[ΗΗ]ΔΔΤΤΧΓΗΔΔΔΔΗΗΙΙC.

Every intervening amount between these two figures is epigraphically impossible, because it cannot be made to agree with the numerals still preserved on the stone.

If now we can prove that the maximum amount possible for this year was *lower* than 222 Tal. 1642 $\frac{5}{12}$ Dr., we shall have established the fact that the only restoration possible is that of the amount mentioned above:

[ΗΓΔΔ]ΔΔΤΤΧΓΗΔΔΔΔΗΗΙΙC.

This proof is possible, if we consider the relation of the separate sums total of the individual years from 426 to 422 to the grand sum total of the payments for all four years.

Whatever the restoration of the final figures for the total of the first year, we know that the sum of the payments of the first and second years equaled 391 Tal. 5600 Dr., which sum is correct within 300 Dr. And whatever the figures to be restored at the end of the total payment for all four years, we know that the amount was 747 Tal. 1000 Dr. which sum is correct within 4000 Dr.

By subtraction we may determine that the combined sums of the 3rd and 4th years amounted to 355 Tal. 1400 Dr., which sum is correct within 5000 Dr. at the most. So far we have succeeded in determining the minimum amount for the fourth year. We must now try to discover the maximum and minimum amounts for the third year, and in this way we shall arrive at the determination for the maximum amount of the fourth year. At first glance the problem looks extremely difficult, for there is preserved in the record of the third year part only of the numeral which gives the amount of the second payment in that year (line 30). But the inscription offers more evidence than is at first apparent, and we make our approach to the problem by studying the amounts of interest preserved throughout the four year period.

For the sake of uniformity we shall consider 40 and 33 as possible maximum and minimum numbers of days in a prytany, where the reckoning of such lengths of prytany is necessary, although again we have chosen limits more widely divergent than necessary for the sake of safety in argument.

The sum total of the interest for the first year is now known to us as 11 Tal. 199 $\frac{1}{6}$ Dr. (p. 35), and the sum total of interest for the fourth year is perfectly preserved in the inscription (line 48) as 1 Tal. 813 $\frac{3}{12}$ Dr. We have no trace on the stone of the amount of interest for the third year, and the amount for the second year can be reckoned only approximately. It is possible, however, in the manner outlined above, to determine a maximum and a minimum amount.

We know, for example, that the first payment of the second year (30 Tal.) was made on the third day of the fourth prytany and that it was outstanding 985 days. The second payment of the second year was made on the fifteenth day of the ninth prytany. If we assume 40 days each for the intervening prytanies, we determine the *minimum* number of days on which interest was computed; if we assume 33 days each for the intervening prytanies we determine the *maximum* number of days for which interest was reckoned. The maximum and minimum numbers of days determined in this way are 808 and 773 respectively. Since 100 Tal. (the amount of the payment) yields 20 Dr. in one day, the maximum interest on the second payment was *2 Tal. 4160 Dr.*; the minimum interest was *2 Tal. 3460 Dr.* The exact interest on the first payment is known, and so the total maximum and minimum of interest for the second year may be easily computed:

	Maximum	Minimum
Interest on Payment I	5910 Dr.	5910 Dr.
Interest on Payment II	2 Tal. 4160 Dr.	2 Tal. 3460 Dr.
Total	3 Tal. 4070 Dr.	3 Tal. 3370 Dr.

We are now in a position to determine also the total maximum and minimum amounts for the combined first, second, and fourth years:

	Maximum		Minimum	
Year I	11 Tal.	199 $\frac{1}{6}$ Dr.	11 Tal.	199 $\frac{1}{6}$ Dr.
Year II	3 Tal.	4070 Dr.	3 Tal.	3370 Dr.
Year IV	1 Tal.	813 $\frac{3}{12}$ Dr.	1 Tal.	813 $\frac{3}{12}$ Dr.
Total	15 Tal.	5082 $\frac{5}{12}$ Dr.	15 Tal.	4382 $\frac{5}{12}$ Dr.

The sum total of interest for all four years is recorded on the stone in line 51 as [Δ]ΓТТТΧΧΧΓΗΗΗΗΔΔΔΓ[– – –, which sum is complete within 5 drachmae.

By subtraction we may compute the possible maximum and minimum of interest for the third year also:

Total for 4 years	max.	18 Tal. 3940 Dr.	min.	18 Tal. 3935 Dr.
Years I, II, and IV	min.	15 Tal. 4382 Dr.	max.	15 Tal. 5083 Dr.
Interest for Year III	max.	2 Tal. 5558 Dr.	min.	2 Tal. 4852 Dr.

When we now consider the amounts of interest for the separate payments made in the third year, we discover that the amounts for the first and third payments are preserved on the stone in their entirety. We may reckon also a possible maximum and minimum of interest on the second payment as well. The amount of this principal is in large part preserved on the stone and we may see at once that it represents a maximum of 25 Tal. and a minimum of 23 Tal. The payment was made on the 12th day of the prytany, but the name and number of the prytanizing tribe are not preserved.

We know, however, that the payment was not made in the first prytany, because the first payment was made on the 26th day of the first prytany (cf. p. 19) and we must assume that the second payment was made at least as late as the second prytany in order to preserve the correct chronological sequence. We know also that the payment was not made as late as the seventh prytany, because Erechtheis held either the 6th or 7th prytany (line 31) and the restoration ἐπὶ τὲς Ἐρεχθεΐδος πρυτανείας ἑβδόμες πρυτανευόσες does not fulfill the requirements of the stoichedon order in lines 29 and 30. The payment was made, therefore, in either prytany II, III, IV, V, or VI.

In the previous year we have already observed that the third day of the fourth prytany was 985 days before the terminus to which interest was reckoned. It follows that the twelfth day of the same prytany was 976 days before the same terminus, and we may determine the maximum number of days for the second payment in 424-3 by assuming that since this date (976 days) 8 prytanies of 33 days each had elapsed; we determine the minimum number of days by assuming that 12 prytanies of 40 days each had elapsed.

$$976 - 264 = 712 \text{ maximum}$$
$$976 - 480 = 496 \text{ minimum}$$

The maximum amount of interest will be reckoned on 25 talents for the period of 712 days; the minimum amount of interest will be reckoned on 23 talents for the period of 496 days.

25 Tal.   in one day yields 5   Dr.
in 712 days yields $5 \times 712 = 3560$ Dr. maximum
23 Tal.   in one day yields 4.6 Dr.
in 496 days yields $4.6 \times 496 = 2281.6$ Dr. maximum

We now know the maximum and minimum amounts of interest for the combined 1st, 2nd, and 3rd payments.

	Maximum	Minimum
Payment I	$4665 \frac{5}{6}$ Dr.	$4665 \frac{5}{6}$ Dr.
Payment II	3560 Dr.	2281 Dr.
Payment III	$632 \frac{3}{12}$ Dr.	$632 \frac{3}{12}$ Dr.
Total	1 Tal. $2858 \frac{1}{12}$ Dr.	1 Tal. $1579 \frac{1}{12}$ Dr.

Since the maximum and minimum amounts for the interest on the whole four payments have already been determined as 2 Tal. 5558 Dr. and 2 Tal. 4852 Dr. respectively, we may determine also the maximum and minimum amounts of interest on the fourth payment alone in 424-3.

Total interest on 4 payments	max. 2 Tal. 5558 Dr.	min. 2 Tal. 4852 Dr.
Interest on payments I, II, III,	min. 1 Tal. 1579 Dr.	max. 1 Tal. 2859 Dr.
Interest on payment IV	max. 1 Tal. 3979 Dr.	min. 1 Tal. 1993 Dr.

The amount of principal of the fourth payment has not been preserved but we know that the payment was made on the 30th day of the prytany, whatever the number of that prytany may have been. It cannot have been made in the 6th prytany for the restoration Ἐρεχθεΐδος— — — ηέϰτες does not agree with the *stoichedon* order of the letters in line 33, and it follows that the payment was made in the 7th, 8th, 9th, or 10th prytany, on the 30th day.

The maximum number of days for this payment is given by reckoning each prytany from here to the terminus, the last day of the last prytany of the following year, as 40 days; and the minimum number of days is given by reckoning each prytany as 33 days. For the maximum calculation we must allow 13 intervening prytanies and 11 days at the end of the prytany in question, and for the minimum calculation we must allow 10 intervening prytanies and 4 days at the end of the prytany in question.

$$\text{Maximum} \quad 13 \times 40 + 11 = 520 + 11 = 533 \text{ days}$$
$$\text{Minimum} \quad 10 \times 33 + 4 = 330 + 4 = 334 \text{ days}$$

We know already the maximum and minimum amounts of interest and the maximum and minimum amounts of principal may be calculated. The maximum amount of principal will be calculated on the maximum amount of interest for the shortest period of time; and the minimum amount of principal will be calculated on the minimum amount of interest for the longest period of time.

For the maximum principal the computation is as follows:

30000 Dr.   in 334 days yields 334 Dr.

x Dr.   in 334 days yields 1 Tal. 3979 Dr. = 9979 Dr.

Algebraically:

$$334x = 30000 \times 9979 = 299370000$$
$$x = 896318 \text{ Dr.} \quad = 149 \text{ Tal. } 2318 \text{ Dr.}$$

For the minimum principal the computation is as follows:

30000 Dr.   in 533 days yields 533 Dr.

x Dr.   in 533 days yields 1 Tal. 1993 Dr. = 7993 Dr.

Algebraically:

$$533x = 30000 \times 7993 = 239790000$$
$$x = 449887 \text{ Dr.} \quad = 74 \text{ Tal. } 5887 \text{ Dr.}$$

In a similar way the maximum and minimum possible amounts for the first payment may be determined. We have shown reasons above for believing that this payment was made during the first prytany (p. 19), but for the sake of argument we assume here that the first payment may have been made in either the 1st, 2nd, 3rd, 4th, or 5th prytany. It cannot have been made in the 6th prytany, because, as we have seen

(p. 42), the latest possible date for the second payment is in the sixth prytany, and in order that the proper chronological sequence may be preserved, we must agree that the first payment fell in one of the prytanies earlier than the sixth.

We know that the payment was made on the 26th day of the prytany, and we know also that the 26th day of the fourth prytany in the previous year was 962 days before the terminus to which interest was reckoned (for the 3rd day of the fourth prytany was 985 days before this terminus). If we reckon seven intervening prytanies of 33 days each we shall obtain the maximum number of days for the first payment in 424-3, and if we reckon 11 intervening prytanies of 40 days each we shall obtain the minimum number of days for which the payment was outstanding:

$$\text{Maximum} \quad 962 - 7 \times 33 = 962 - 231 = 731 \text{ days}$$
$$\text{Minimum} \quad 962 - 11 \times 40 = 962 - 440 = 522 \text{ days}$$

The amount of interest is known as $4665 \frac{5}{6}$ Dr., and the possible amounts of principal may be determined as follows:

1. 30000 Dr. in 522 days yields 522 Dr.
    x Dr. in 522 days yields $4665 \frac{5}{6}$ Dr.

Algebraically:
$$522x = 30000 \times 4665 \frac{5}{6} = 139975000$$
$$x = 268152 \text{ Dr.} = 44 \text{ Tal. } 4152 \text{ Dr.} \quad \text{Maximum amount}$$

2. 30000 Dr. in 731 days yields 731 Dr.
    x Dr. in 731 days yields $4665 \frac{5}{6}$ Dr.

Algebraically:
$$731x = 30000 \times 4665 \frac{5}{6} = 139975000$$
$$x = 191484 \text{ Dr.} = 31 \text{ Tal. } 5484 \text{ Dr.} \quad \text{Minimum amount}$$

For the second payment the maximum and minimum amounts are already known as 25 Tal. and 23 Tal. respectively.

The interest on the third payment is known as $632 \frac{1}{4}$ Dr., and the payment fell in the 6th or 7th prytany. The maximum number of days is obtained if we reckon 15 prytanies of 40 days each to the terminus to which interest was computed, and the minimum number of days is obtained if we reckon 13 prytanies of 33 days each.

$$\text{Maximum} \quad 15 \times 40 = 600 \text{ days}$$
$$\text{Minimum} \quad 13 \times 33 = 429 \text{ days}$$

The maximum and minimum amounts of principal may now be determined as above:

    1.   30000 Dr. in 429 days yields 429 Dr.

            x Dr. in 429 days yields $632 \frac{1}{4}$ Dr.

Algebraically:

$$429x = 30000 \times 632 \tfrac{1}{4} = 18967500$$
$$x = 44214 \text{ Dr.} = 7 \text{ Tal. } 2214 \text{ Dr.} \qquad \text{Maximum}$$

    2.   30000 Dr. in 600 days yields 600 Dr.

            x Dr. in 600 days yields $632 \frac{1}{4}$ Dr.

Algebraically:

$$600x = 30000 \times 632 \tfrac{1}{4} = 18967500$$
$$x = 31612 \text{ Dr.} = 5 \text{ Tal. } 1612 \text{ Dr.} \qquad \text{Minimum}$$

We may now add the total amounts of principal as determined for this year to obtain the total possible maximum and minimum amounts for the four combined payments:

	Maximum	Minimum
Payment I	44 Tal. 4152 Dr.	31 Tal. 5484 Dr.
Payment II	25 Tal.	23 Tal.
Payment III	7 Tal. 2214 Dr.	5 Tal. 1612 Dr.
Payment IV	149 Tal. 2318 Dr.	74 Tal. 5887 Dr.
Total (424 - 3)	226 Tal. 2684 Dr.	135 Tal. 983 Dr.

We have observed above (p. 40) that the combined totals of the third and fourth years amounted to 355 Tal. 1400 Dr., which sum was correct within 5000 Dr.

By subtracting from this figure the maximum possible sum for the principal of the third year, we find that the minimum possible sum of principal in the fourth year was 128 Tal. 4716 Dr. This determination is of no direct value, however, because we have already discovered that the minimum possible sum for the fourth year was 192 Tal. $1642 \frac{5}{12}$ Dr. (cf. p. 40 above).

But by subtracting from the sum total of the combined third and fourth years the minimum possible payment of the third year, we find that the maximum possible amount of principal in the fourth year was 220 Tal. 417 Dr., which sum is correct within 5000 Dr.

    335 Tal. 1400 Dr.   (correct within 5000 Dr.)

    135 Tal.   983 Dr.

    220 Tal.   417 Dr.   (correct within 5000 Dr.)

This figure is of the greatest importance, because it means that the restoration of the sum total of the principal of the fourth year as *222* odd talents is impossible, and the figures preserved on the stone allow only one alternative. The restoration must be

[HⴖΔΔ]ΔΔTTXⴖHΔΔΔΔⱵⱵIIC.

This is a step forward of considerable significance in the restoration of the document, and its immediate consequence is that the sum total of payments made during the third year must be restored as 163 talents. This numeral, it may be observed, exactly fills the space available for it on the stone in line 35.

Indeed, the way is now clear toward determining the exact amount in each case where the sum total of money borrowed from Athena Polias is recorded in the inscription. We have the following data with which to deal:

First Year	HHⴖΔTⴖⴖH[. ³ .]	line 15
Second Year	H[ΔΔΔ]	line 23
Third Year	[HⴖΔTTT]	line 35
Fourth Year	[HⴖΔΔ]ΔΔTTXⴖHΔΔΔΔⱵⱵIIC	line 47
Total Four Years	[ⴖ]HHΔΔΔΔⴖTTX[. . .⁶. . .]	line 49
Total of Previous Seven Years, written in Words	✗✗✗✗TXXXXⴖΔΔⱵⱵ	lines 99-100
Total for Eleven Years	✗✗✗✗ⴖHHΔΔΔΔⴖTTTⴖⴖH[. .⁵. .]	line 114

I submit the following as the only possible combination which satisfies the requirements of the stone:

First Year	HHⴖΔTⴖⴖH[ΔIIIC]	line 15
Second Year	H[ΔΔΔ]	line 23
Third Year	[HⴖΔTTT]	line 35
Fourth Year	[HⴖΔΔ]ΔΔTTXⴖHΔΔΔΔⱵⱵIIC	line 47
Total Four Years	[ⴖ]HHΔΔΔΔⴖTTX[HHⴖⱵⱵⱵ]	line 49
Total of Previous Seven Years, written in Words	✗✗✗✗TXXXXⴖΔΔⱵⱵ	lines 99-100
Total for Eleven Years	✗✗✗✗ⴖHHΔΔΔΔⴖTTTⴖⴖH[HⴖΔΔⴖ]	line 114

These restorations are embodied in the transcript (Plate II).

CHAPTER V

THE ACCOUNTS OF ATHENA NIKE

We have been discussing so far the various total amounts of money borrowed from the treasury of Athena Polias, but at this point it will be useful to turn our attention also to the records of money borrowed from Athena Nike.

In lines 106-108 I have restored the amount of principal computed in the previous seven years as εἴκοσι ταλάντοις δυοῖν ταλ[άντοιν τρισχιλίαις ἐνενέκον]τα δραχμ[αῖς] ὀκτὸ [δραχ]μαῖς δυοῖν ὀβολοῖν. This sum yielded as interest throughout the quadrennium from 426 to 422 ΤΓΗΡΔΔΔΔΗΙΙ[– – – , with the possibility that some few obols have been lost from the end of the numeral.

Kubicki's suggested restoration (*cf. Editio Minor* of the *Corpus,* Vol. I, p. 155) differs from mine in having [ὀγδοέκον]τα in place of [ἐνενέκον]τα in line 108, and though it has been accepted as certain by Unger, as a matter of fact either restoration is possible so far as the amount of the interest is concerned, and both are epigraphically correct (*cf.* Plate I). We shall see reason shortly for preferring the restoration [ἐνενέκον]τα, which gives as the amount of interest approximately ΤΓΗΡΔΔΔΔΗΙΙ[ΙΙΙ].

This total amount of *22 Tal. 3098 Dr. 2 obols* must be added to the payment recorded in line 53 to give the total in line 112:

Payment in lines 106-108		ΔΔΤΤΧΧΧΓΔΔΔΔΠΗΗΗΙΙ
Payment in line	53	[..] or [.] (depending on whether line 52 has 74 or 75 letters)
Total in line 112		ΔΔΓΤΤΤΧΧΧΓΔΔΔΔΠΗΗΗΙΙ

It is obvious that the amount to be restored in line 53 is 6 Tal. 450 Dr. and this sum is written in Greek numerical characters as ΓΤΗΗΗΗΓ, but it is equally obvious that this restoration is impossible, because there are at most two spaces available for it on the stone.

For a time I had thought that the payment from the treasure of Hermes might have been included in the grand total of the treasure of Athena Nike, and that the amount (One Talent and 490 Dr.) might have been added to the sum in line 53 and the sum in lines 106-108 to give the total in line 112. In this case the numeral in line 53 might be restored as [Ͱ], which is entirely possible, and the numeral in lines 106-108 might be restored as *22 Tal. 3058 Dr. 2 obols.* The total amount in line 112 would then be obtained by the following addition:

Athena Nike in 7 years	22 Tal.	3058 Dr.	2 obols
Athena Nike in 4 years	5 Tal.		
Hermes in 7 years	1 Tal.	490 Dr.	

Athena Nike and Hermes in 11 years 28 Tal.   3548 Dr.   2 obols.

But this explanation involves the assumption that between 426 and 422 the treasures of Athena Nike and of Hermes were amalgamated, and furthermore we are unable to reckon the interest on *22 Tal. 3058 Dr. 2 obols* in such a way as to give in 1464 days the amount of interest preserved on the stone. This is true whether we reckon with the use of decimal notation, or with the use of the tables given above (pp. 32 and 34). As a possible explanation the hypothesis must, I believe, be discarded.

Our only recourse is to assume that in fact the amounts of lines 106-108 and of line 53 were added to give the amount in line 112. This is possible only in case there was some error on the part of the stonecutter in copying the latter amount, or some error on the part of the auditors in making the reckoning. I restore [ἐνενέκον]τα in line 108, and give the numeral in line 53 as [ͰT]. Both of these restorations are epigraphically satisfactory. In reckoning the sum total, however, we must assume that the numeral Ͱ was written in line 112 instead of the numeral Ͱ.

The addition is as follows:

Lines 106-108 ΔΔΤΤΧΧΧͰΔΔΔΔΠͰͰͰΙΙ (expressed in words)

Line   53   [ͰT]

Line   112   ΔΔͰΤΤΤΧΧΧ(Ͱ)ΔΔΔΔΠͰͰͰΙΙ

Such errors of the stonecutter are not without parallel, and I may cite by way of example the numeral ΗͰͰ which is given as the tithe from the tribute of Μυέσσιοι in *I.G.* I², 193, Col. II, line 30 (*cf.* Meritt and West, The Reconstruction of *I.G.* I², 193, 194, and 201, *Transactions and Proceedings of the American Philological Association,*

Vol. LVI, 1925, plate facing p. 253) where the correct reading is obviously ⊢ℙ. The error in the reverse direction appears, I suspect, in the tithe from the tribute recorded in *I.G.* I², 198, Col. II, line 23 (*cf.* Meritt and West, A Revision of Athenian Tribute Lists, *Harvard Studies in Classical Philology*, Vol. 37, 1926, plate facing p. 70) where the numeral appears on the stone as ℙ and the restoration should be (ℙ) [Κνίδιοι].

In the present instance, however, we have to deal not with an error of the stonecutter, but with an error made by the auditors themselves, for a mere error in transcription could not have become involved in the reckoning of further sums, so as to appear also in the items of lines 114 ff. But the item in line 116 is such that we know the auditors must have reckoned in the numeral of line 112 as it is actually given on the stone, and the fault in addition must be charged to them rather than to the stonecutter.

The already complicated problems of this inscription are rendered still more complex by the knowledge that the reckonings of the auditors were not infallible. We shall have occasion to recur to this later.

We have observed above (p. 47) that the amount of principal loaned by Athena Polias during the eleven years was ✕✕✕✕ℙⱵⱵ△△△△ℙТТТℙℙⱵ[ℙ△△ℾ] and this numeral has been restored in line 114. We may add to this the amount of the sum total of principal borrowed from Athena Nike, recorded in line 112, and the restoration of line 116 is determined as [✕✕✕✕]ℙⱵⱵℙ△△ℾТТ✕✕✕ⱵⱵ[Ⱶ△△⊢⊢⊢⊦⊦].

This represents the sum total borrowed from Athena Nike and Athena Polias in the eleven years from 433 to 422.

------ ••• ------

CHAPTER VI

___

SINGLE PAYMENTS FROM THE TREASURE OF ATHENA POLIAS

We have dealt so far with total sums of interest and of principal and have succeeded in establishing the amounts paid from the treasure of Athena Polias in each of the four years from 426-5 to 423-2. This determination has been made possible by mathematical computations in maxima and minima, and the restorations involved may be considered as mathematically certain.

The major problems connected with the inscription, however, are the restoration of the individual amounts of payment within the several years, the determination of the amounts of interest accrued on these payments, and the determination also of the dates on which the several payments were made. Many conditions have to be satisfied in the course of this study, for all determinations must be epigraphically possible and must conform to the limitations of the *stoichedon* order of the letters on the stone. All individual sums must be such as to give the sums total we have already determined; and the amounts of interest at the same time must add to equal the individual yearly totals of interest, which in turn must yield the grand sum total for all four years, the significant figures of which are preserved on the stone. The last and perhaps the most significant check on any solution attained is that the dates of the various payments must take their place in logical order in some comprehensible scheme of the calendar year.

It is readily apparent, I am sure, that the difficulty will not be in finding too many solutions which fashion themslves into this complex and yet consistent whole. The difficulty will be in finding any set of restorations which satisfy at the same time all the given conditions.

The dates on which payments were made are given by the so-called senatorial calendar, in which the year was divided into ten prytanies named after the prytanizing tribes, whose order of precedence through the year was determined by lot (*cf.* Ferguson, The Athenian Secretaries, *Cornell Studies in Classical Philology*, No. VII, 1898, p. 26). Dates of payments made by the Other Gods are given, however, not only by the senatorial year, but also by the civil year, and we have found in line 79 a valuable cross-reference between the two systems of dating in the statement that the 23ʳᵈ day of Skirophorion, 423-2, was the same as the 20ᵗʰ day of the tenth prytany. This in itself is sufficient to show that the senatorial year was not equated with the civil year, though we know also from the fact that our quadrennium of senatorial years contained 1464 days that no combination of four civil years can be made to correspond to it. The elaborate scheme evolved by Keil to show the correspondences between the two calendars we have proved invalid, and we must if possible find evidence for a new comparative table in this inscription.

Very few of the records of payments made from Athena's money are preserved in such a way that we may be certain as to the date of the prytany when the payment was made and also as to the number of days for which the payment was outstanding. What slight evidence there is, however, points to prytanies of 36 or 37 days.[1]

The first payment, for example, was made on the fourth day of the second prytany in 426-5, and was outstanding for 1424 days. The first day of the second prytany, therefore, fell 1427 days before the end of the quadrennium, and the first prytany must have contained 1464 1427 37 days.

If we restore hεπτὰ at the end of line 6 we find also that the second prytany contained 37 days, for the amounts of interest show that 27 days had elapsed between the first and second payments, and that the second payment was made on the 31ˢᵗ day of the prytany. If seven days were still reckoned at the end of the prytany, that prytany contained 37 days.

We have seen above (p. 36) that the restoration δέκα is necessary at the end of line 11 and we know that the fifth payment was outstanding for 1197 days. Since the payment was made on the tenth day of the eighth prytany, the first day of the eighth prytany was 1206 days before the end of the quadrennium. If we assign 37 days to each of the first 6 prytanies of this year, and 36 days to the seventh prytany, we find that the first day of the eighth prytany does actually fall 1206 days before the terminus to which interest was reckoned.

$$1464 - (6 \times 37 + 36) \quad 1464 - 258 - 1206.$$

This arrangement of prytanies suggests immediately the scheme followed in

[1] *Cf.* also below, Chap. IX, Part I.

the fourth century (*c/. Aristotle, Constitution of Athens, 43, 2*) whereby the first four prytanies contained 36 days each and the last six contained 35 days each. At this time, of course, the senatorial year was equated with the civil year and the total number of days was 354. This coincidence between the two calendars had not been effected in the fifth century, and yet it may be a significant thought that the senatorial year was made up, let us say, of six prytanies of 37 days each followed by four prytanies of 36 days each. In actual application there might be some variation in the order of 36 and 37 day prytanies, just as we know from the inscriptions of the fourth century that the succession of prytanies did not always fall as Aristotle indicates.

This hypothesis seems the more probable when we realize that a senatorial year composed in this way contains 366 days. We know that the quadrennium contained 1464 days, and this number is divisible by 366 exactly four times.

Let us assume, then, temporarily, that the first day of the first prytany in 425-4 fell 366 days after the first day of the first prytany in 426-5 and consequently 1098 days before the terminus to which interest was reckoned. We know that the first payment of the second year was made on the third day of the fourth prytany and that it was outstanding for 985 days. This time relation is possible if the first three prytanies of 425-4 contained 37 days each.

For the third and fourth years, unfortunately, in the record of moneys borrowed from Athena direct evidence in support of the proposed succession of prytanies is as yet lacking. Only in the second payment made from the treasure of the Other Gods in the year 423-2 do we find that the 20th day of the tenth prytany fell 17 days before the end of the quadrennium. This last prytany, therefore, contained 36 days, and conforms to the hypothesis which has been outlined above.

We may add to the evidence above the fact that the years 408-7 and 407-6 also contained prytanies of 36 and 37 days, as indicated below in Chap. IX, Part I.

Some of these observations I had made before arriving at the proof that the sum total of the principal borrowed from Athena in the fourth year was [ℍℙΔΔ]ΔΔΤΤΧℙℍΔΔΔΔⱵⱵⅠⅠC. Curiously enough, this determination fixes also the date of the first payment made in that year as 355 days before the end of the quadrennium. The proof of this is somewhat complex, and we shall devote ourselves to that problem below, but it is important here to notice that the only possible restoration for the date of this payment brings it to the 11th day of the first prytany. By reckoning back we discover that the fourth year of the quadrennium contained 365 days, which is a very close approximation to the theoretical 366 days which our interpretation of the senatorial year has indicated.

The above observations cannot be urged as proof that the prytanies contained 36 and 37 days in such sequence that each senatorial year contained approximately 366 days. And yet I think they make such an assumption highly probable and point the way which we should follow in our subsequent investigation. If we find that the various amounts of principal and interest can all be restored so as to give the proper dates and sums total on the assumption outlined above, then, however, I think that assumption may be taken as an established fact, at least in its main outlines, and the most serious part of our problem will have been solved.

We have already determined that the maximum and minimum amounts which may be restored for the principal of the first payment in 424-3 fall between 45 and 31 Talents (*cf.* p. 45) and we know that no figure between these limits can occupy the 32 spaces on the stone between the word πρυτανείας toward the end of line 28, and the word τόκος which must be restored in line 29. We must restore after the word πρυτανείας some such phrase as ἐχς Ὀπισθοδόμο, on the analogy of lines 19-20. Even so there are left 19 letter spaces to be filled by the numeral which represents the amount of the first payment.

We have already shown that this payment was made during the first prytany, and the date within the prytany, εἰκοστῖι καὶ ἡέκτει, is preserved on the stone. Now under the assumption that the first day of the first prytany in this year was 732 days before the end of the quadrennium, the 26th day of the first prytany gives 707 as the number of days on which interest was reckoned. With the amount of the interest known it is possible at once to compute the amount of the principal.

$$30000 \text{ Dr. in 707 days yields } 707 \text{ Dr.}$$
$$x \text{ Dr. in 707 days yields } 4665 \tfrac{5}{6} \text{ Dr.}$$

Algebraically:

$$707x = 30000 \times 4665 \tfrac{5}{6} = 139975000$$
$$x = 197984 \text{ Dr.} = 32 \text{ Tal. } 5984 \text{ Dr.}$$

This amount of principal is expressed in Greek notation as

ΔΔΔΤΤ𐅅𐅄ΗΗΗΗ𐅅ΔΔΔⅠⅠⅠ,

and it is worthy of notice that the numeral occupies exactly the nineteen spaces which are available for it on the stone. We may work back from this amount of principal, of course, to obtain the amount of interest preserved on the stone, and the result is not materially changed whether we use the decimal system of notation or the table suggested above on p. 32.

Working from the table:

30 Tal.	in 707 days yields	4242 Dr.
2 Tal. 5500 Dr.	in one day yields $3\frac{1}{2}$ obols	
	in 707 days yields $2474\frac{1}{2}$ obols $= 412$ Dr. $2\frac{1}{2}$ ob.	
484 Dr.	in one day yields	

$$\frac{484}{1250} \times \frac{1}{4} = \frac{121}{1250}\,\text{obol} = \frac{1}{12} + \frac{1}{72}\,\text{obol}$$

in 707 days $59 + 9\frac{1}{2} = 68\frac{1}{2}$ obols $=$ 11 Dr. $2\frac{1}{2}$ ob.

---

32 Tal. 5984 Dr.	in 707 days yields	4665 Dr. 5 obols.

But we may leave this for a moment and proceed to the amount of the third payment. As we have seen (p. 27) this numeral ends in 200 Dr. We know also that the payment was made during the 6th or 7th prytany, and in order to have the principal in correct proportion to the amount of the interest preserved on the stone, we must restore the numeral, whatever the number of the prytany, as approximately 6 Tal.

We already know that the amount of the second payment was between 23 Tal. and 25 Tal., and that the sum total of the four payments was 163 Tal. (p. 47).

These figures for the sum total and for the amounts of the first three payments indicate also the amount of the fourth payment, and *it is approximately 100 Talents*. This, I feel sure, is more than a coincidence, and it gives assurance that the investigation is proceeding in the right direction. For we know that a payment of 100 Tal. was made in each of the other three years of the quadrennium, toward the end of the year. In the first year the payment was made in the 8th prytany, in the second year in the 9th prytany, and in the fourth year in the 8th prytany — as will appear below. We may restore, I think with certainty, the amount of the principal of the fourth payment in 424-3 as ⊢, and conclude that the payment was made on the 30th day of the eighth prytany (*cf.* also Chap. IX, Part I below). Assuming that the fourth year contained 365 days (*cf.* p. 53) and that the last three prytanies of 424-3 contained respectively 37, 36, and 36 days, the payment fell 445 days before the terminus to which interest was reckoned. Interest on 100 Tal. in 445 days amounts to 8900 Dr., and we should restore lines 33-34 as follows:

— — τριακοστῆι τῆς πρυταν[είας ⊢ τόκος
τούτοις ἐγένετο ΤΧΧℙΗΗΗΗ𐅵𐅵 κεφάλαιον] — —

It may be observed that this restoration fulfills perfectly the requirements of the stone. The number of days for which interest was reckoned cannot have been greater than 445 without giving an amount of interest epigraphically impossible, and the first possible amount of interest lower than that proposed would necessitate the assumption that at least one of the last three prytanies of 424-3 contained only 35 days.

Since we know that the numeral representing the third payment in this year ended in two 100-drachmae signs, and that the payment was made during either the sixth or seventh prytany (Plate I, line 31), we may reckon without great difficulty the various possible amounts of principal which yield as interest the amount $632\frac{1}{4}$ Dr. preserved on the stone, while allowing at the same time a restoration of the date of payment which conforms to the sequence of 36 and 37 day prytanies. The possibilities are exactly four, as follows:

1.   5 Tal. 4800 Dr. in 545 days yields $632\frac{1}{4}$ Dr.
     The date is the 3rd day of the 6th prytany.

2.   5 Tal. 5900 Dr. in 528 days yields $632\frac{1}{4}$ Dr.
     The date is the 20th day of the 6th prytany.

3.   6 Tal.   700 Dr. in 517 days yields $632\frac{1}{4}$ Dr.
     The date is the 30th day of the 6th prytany.

4.   6 Tal. 1200 Dr. in 510 days yields $632\frac{1}{4}$ Dr.
     The date is the 2nd day of the 7th prytany.

These figures must be considered in connection with the possible amounts of principal for the first payment, made on the 26th day of the first prytany. Assuming prytanies of 36 and 37 days throughout the year 425-4 as well as 424-3, these approximate amounts of principal (irrespective at present of their epigraphical possibilities) are as follows:

a.   32 Tal. 5700 Dr. in 708 days yields $4665\frac{5}{6}$ Dr.
b.   32 Tal. 5984 Dr. in 707 days yields $4665\frac{5}{6}$ Dr.
c.   33 Tal.   265 Dr. in 706 days yields $4665\frac{5}{6}$ Dr.
d.   33 Tal.   546 Dr. in 705 days yields $4665\frac{5}{6}$ Dr.
e.   33 Tal.   828 Dr. in 704 days yields $4665\frac{5}{6}$ Dr.
f.   33 Tal. 1111 Dr. in 703 days yields $4665\frac{5}{6}$ Dr.

To obtain these figures it is necessary to allow the interest period on the second payment of 425-4 to vary from 793 to 788 days, and the epigraphical possibilities for the restoration of the amount of interest reduce the number of possibilities still further to 793, 791, 790, or 788 days.

Since the total amounts of interest in the fourth and first years are definitely known, and since we know also three of the four individual amounts of interest in the third year and also the sum total of interest for all four years (within 5 Dr.), these four possible restorations for the interest on the second payment of the second year determine at once four possible restorations for the amount of interest on the second payment of the third year, as follows:

I   2955 + Dr. (within 5 Dr.)

II   2995 + Dr. (within 5 Dr.)

III   3015 + Dr. (within 5 Dr.)

IV   3055 + Dr. (within 5 Dr.)

We may now see what combination of amount of principal on the third payment with amount of principal on the first payment gives an amount of principal for the second payment which will yield one of the mathematically possible amounts of interest. Fortunately we know that the payment was made on the 12th day of the prytany, and experiment shows that it is necessary to consider only the 3rd and 4th prytanies in determining the possibilities.

It would be tedious and unnecessary here to give all the computations involved. I have considered as possible interest periods for the third prytany 644-648 days, and for the fourth prytany 607-611 days. The following solutions appear as mathematically possible:

A. Possibility (1) for the third payment and possibility (a) for the first payment give a principal of 24 Tal. 1500 Dr. for the 2nd payment, which in 610 days (fourth prytany) yields interest of approximately 2958.5 Dr. (Possibility I above).

B. Possibility (1) for the third payment and possibility (b) for the first payment give a principal of 24 Tal. 1216 Dr. for the 2nd payment, which in 611 days (fourth prytany) yields interest of approximately 2957.5 Dr. (Possibility I above).

C. Possibility (4) for the third payment and possibility (c) for the first payment give a principal of 23 Tal. 4535 Dr. for the 2nd payment, which in 644 days (third prytany) yields interest of approximately 3059.7 Dr. (Possibility IV above).

D. Possibility (4) for the third payment and possibility (d) for the first payment give a principal of 23 Tal. 4254 Dr. for the 2nd payment, which in 645 days (third prytany) yields interest of approximately 3058 Dr. (Possibility IV above).

E. Possibility (3) for the third payment and possibility (e) for the first payment give a principal of 23 Tal. 4472 Dr. for the 2nd payment, which in 644 days (third prytany) yields interest of approximately 3058 Dr. (Possibility IV above).

F. Possibility (4) for the third payment and possibility (e) for the first payment give a principal of 23 Tal. 3972 Dr. for the 2ⁿᵈ payment, which in 646 days (third prytany) yields interest of approximately 3057 Dr. (Possibility IV above).

G.   Possibility (3) for the third payment and possibility (f) for the first payment give a principal of 23 Tal. 4190 Dr. for the 2ⁿᵈ payment, which in 645 days (third prytany) yields interest of approximately 3057 Dr. (Possibility IV above).

H.   Possibility (4) for the third payment and possibility (f) for the first payment give a principal of 23 Tal. 3690 Dr. for the 2ⁿᵈ payment, which in 647 days (third prytany) yields interest of approximately 3055.7 Dr. (Possibility IV above).

Of these eight solutions, A–H, all mathematically possible:

A necessitates that one of the first three prytanies of 424-3 shall contain 38 days.

B necessitates that one of the last two prytanies of 425-4 shall contain 38 days.

C necessitates that the first two prytanies of 424-3 shall contain 38 days each.

E gives amounts of principal and interest for the 2ⁿᵈ payment of the third year which occupy too many spaces on the stone, and is epigraphically impossible.

F gives amounts of principal and interest for the 2ⁿᵈ payment of the third year which occupy too many spaces on the stone, and is epigraphically impossible.

G is improbable because it necessitates the assumption that 425-4 contained 370 days while 424-3 contained only 363 days.

H necessitates that the first two prytanies of 424-3 shall contain 35 days each, and is further improbable because it necessitates the assumption that 425-4 contained 370 days while 424-3 contained only 363 days.

Solution D, on the other hand, conforms to the calendar scheme which we have been establishing, allowing a regular succession of 36 and 37 day prytanies, and is in every way epigraphically possible. Assuming that it is correct we have the following data for the restoration of the document:

The last payment of the 2ⁿᵈ year was outstanding for 788 days and yielded interest of ΤΤΧΧΧℙΗΗℙΔ. The last two prytanies of 425-4 contained 36 days each, and Pryt. I, 1 of 424-3 fell 730 days before the terminus to which interest was reckoned. The senatorial year 425-4 contained 368 days, and the senatorial year 424-3 (like 423-2) contained 365 days.

The first payment in 424-3, made on the 26ᵗʰ day of the first prytany, was outstanding 705 days. The principal was 33 Tal. 550 Dr., which yielded interest of

4665 $\frac{5}{6}$ Dr. I suggest as a possible restoration before the numeral the words στρατεγοῖς ἐς τὰ ἐπὶ Θράικες which fill the *lacuna* after the word πρυτανείας in line 28.

The first two prytanies of 424-3 contained 37 days each, and the second payment was made on the 12th day of the third prytany, 645 days before the terminus to which interest was reckoned. The principal of 23 Tal. 4250 Dr. yielded interest of 3057 Dr. 5 obols.

The third payment was made on the 2nd day of the seventh prytany and was outstanding for 510 days. The principal of 6 Tal. 1200 Dr. yielded interest of 632 $\frac{1}{4}$ Dr. Entirely apart from mathematical considerations we may note that historical probability favors the restoration of the seventh prytany, rather than the sixth, for the date of this payment. The seventh prytany falls at the beginning of the campaigning season, and we may note that throughout the inscription no payments are recorded during the 5th and 6th prytanies (midwinter).

Amounts of interest on the first three payments in 424-3 may be computed as follows:

First Payment: 33 Tal. 550 Dr. in 705 days (*cf.* table p. 32).

30 Tal.	in one day yields 6 Dr.	
	in 705 days yields	4230 Dr.
2 Tal. 5500 Dr.	in one day yields 3 $\frac{1}{2}$ obols	
	in 705 days yields 3 $\frac{1}{2}$ × 705	
	= 2467 $\frac{1}{2}$ obols	= 411 Dr. 1 $\frac{1}{2}$ obols
1050 Dr.	in one day yields $\frac{1050}{1250}$ × $\frac{1}{4}$ = $\frac{5}{24}$ (approximately) = $\frac{1}{8}$ + $\frac{1}{12}$ ob.	
	in 705 days yields 88 $\frac{1}{8}$ + 59 = 147 $\frac{1}{2}$ ob. app. =	24 Dr. 3 $\frac{1}{8}$ obols

33 Tal. 550 Dr.	in 705 days yields	4665 Dr. 5 obols.

Second Payment: 23 Tal. 4250 Dr. in 645 days (*cf.* table p. 32).

20 Tal.	in one day yields 4 Dr.	
	in 645 days yields	2580 Dr.
3 Tal. 3250 Dr.	in one day yields 4 $\frac{1}{4}$ obols	
	in 645 days yields 4 $\frac{1}{4}$ × 645	
	= 2741 $\frac{1}{4}$ obols	= 456 Dr. 5 $\frac{1}{4}$ obols.
1000 Dr.	in one day yields $\frac{1000}{1250}$ × $\frac{1}{4}$ obol	
	= $\frac{1}{5}$ = $\frac{1}{9}$ + $\frac{1}{12}$ obol (approximately)	
	in 645 days yields 125 $\frac{5}{12}$ obols	20 Dr. 5 $\frac{5}{12}$ obols.

23 Tal. 4250 Dr.	in 645 days yields	3057 Dr. 5 obols.

Third Payment: 6 Tal. 1200 Dr. in 510 days (*cf.* table p. 32)

5 Tal.		in one day yields one Dr.		
		in 510 days yields	510 Dr.	
1 Tal.	250 Dr.	in one day yields $1\frac{1}{4}$ obol		
		in 510 days yields $637\frac{1}{2}$ obols $= 106$ Dr. $1\frac{1}{2}$ obols.		
	950 Dr.	in one day yields $\frac{950}{1250} \times \frac{1}{4}$ obol		
		$\frac{3}{16}$ obols $\frac{1}{8} + \frac{1}{16}$ obols		
		in 510 days yields $64 + 32$ 96 ob. — 16 Dr.		

6 Tal.   1200 Dr.   in 510 days yields   632 Dr. $1\frac{1}{2}$ obols.

We may now add the individual sums of interest on the separate payments of the third year, to determine the sum total, as follows:

Interest on the First	Payment		4665 Dr.	5	obols.
» » » Second	»		3057 Dr.	5	obols.
» » » Third	»		632 Dr.	$1\frac{1}{2}$	obols.
» » » Fourth	»	1 Tal.	2900 Dr.	—	—
Total Interest for 3rd Year		2 Tal.	5255 Dr.	$5\frac{1}{2}$	obols.

This amount may be written in Greek characters as ΤΤⴲΗΗⴲΠΙΙΙΙΙC and should be restored in line 36.

The sums total of interest in each of the four years are now known and these totals may be added to give the sum total of all four years which appears in line 51, as follows:

Interest for the First Year	11 Tal.	199 Dr.	1	obol.
Interest for the Second Year	3 Tal.	3670 Dr.	— —	— —
Interest for the Third Year	2 Tal.	5255 Dr.	$5\frac{1}{2}$	obols.
Interest for the Fourth Year	1 Tal.	813 Dr.	$1\frac{1}{2}$	obols.
Total Interest for Four Years	18 Tal.	3938 Dr.	2	obols.

It is perhaps a curious coincidence that our calendar system has found strong support in the records of the third year, where least is preserved on the stone. Our discussion of the third year has involved also the question of the last payment of the second year, and we now see that every item in the record of these two years may be restored if we assume prytanies of 36 and 37 days. Any doubt that this may be the proper interpretation of the senatorial calendar will be removed, I believe, when we see also that the records of the first and fourth years demand a succession of 36 and 37 day prytanies.

It will be best to undertake first the restoration of the several items in the record of the fourth year, where we have already determined (p. 47) that the sum total of the principal was 192 Tal. 1642 $\frac{5}{12}$ Dr. This determination is of considerable importance here, because it gives to us the proof that the sums of interest preserved for the third payment (line 43) and for the fifth payment (line 46) are in themselves complete, and that no portions of the numerals have been lost by the fracturing of the stone.

We may arrive at this proof in the following way, by adding together the several amounts of principal preserved on the stone, and then by showing that an amount of interest larger than that preserved on the stone for the third or fifth payment would necessitate a corresponding individual amount of principal so high that the sum total would exceed the amount 192 Tal. 1642 $\frac{5}{12}$ Dr. preserved in line 47.

The minimum sum total of principal in the fourth year has already been determined (p. 40) as 187 Tal. 1126 Dr., while the minimum amounts of individual payments were fixed as follows:

Payment I	59 Tal.	4720 Dr.
Payment II	2 Tal.	5500 Dr.
Payment III	9 Tal.	1094 Dr.
Payment IV	100 Tal.	- - - -
Payment V	15 Tal.	1812 Dr.
Minimum Total	187 Tal.	1126 Dr.

The total minimum determined in this way does not exceed the known total of the five payments preserved in line 47 as 192 Tal. 1642 $\frac{5}{12}$ Dr., and a restoration is possible if we consider as complete the numerals preserved on the stone as interest for the third and fifth payments.

If, however, we assume that the amount of interest for the third payment, given in line 43, is not complete, but that the restoration should be [X]ΓΓΔΔΔⱵΙ, then the amount of principal demanded as a minimum by this restoration and calculated on the same basis as above (p. 39) is 24 Tal. 5731 Dr., and the sum total of the individual payments amounts to well over 200 Tal. This is of course impossible and the amount of interest must be considered complete as it stands.

In a similar way we may suppose that the amount of interest preserved on the

stone for the fifth payment is not complete (line 46), but that the restoration should
be [H]HΔΔΑΗΗIIC. The amount of principal demanded as a minimum by this restoration
and calculated in the same way as above (p. 39) is 27 Tal. 4800 Dr., approximately,
and the sum total of the individual payments would in this case also amount to more
than 199 Tal. This restoration is likewise impossible, and the number as it is preserved
on the stone must be considered as complete for the interest on the fifth payment.

Of the five amounts of interest in the record of the fourth year we now know
two exactly, those of the third and fifth payments. The interest on the second
payment may be restored at once, within one obol. If we consider the principal as
ΤΤ⋈⋈, interest would be reckoned in 281 days as H⋈ΔΑΗΗΗIIII[IC], or if we consider
the principal as [Τ]ΤΤ⋈⋈ interest would be reckoned in 209 days as H⋈ΔΗΗΗIIII[C].
There are no other possibilities. The interest on the fourth payment was between
1600 Dr. and 2000 Dr. (line 45) and the total interest of the year is known exactly
as 1 Tal. 813 $\frac{1}{4}$ Dr. (line 48). We have the further knowledge that the amount of
interest on the fourth payment, whatsoever it was, must have been exactly divisible
by 20 (for 100 Tal. yields 20 Dr. a day), and that the numeral which represented the
interest on the first payment occupied on the stone 19 letter spaces (c/. Plate I, line 40).

These considerations are sufficient to determine exactly the amounts of interest
on the first and fourth payments.

We may add together the amounts of interest from payments II, III, and
V as follows:

	Maximum	Minimum
Interest on Payment II	163 $\frac{11}{12}$ Dr.	163 $\frac{9}{12}$ Dr.
Interest on Payment III	582 $\frac{1}{6}$ Dr.	582 $\frac{1}{6}$ Dr.
Interest on Payment V	122 $\frac{5}{12}$ Dr.	122 $\frac{5}{12}$ Dr.
Interest on Payments II, III, and V 868 $\frac{1}{2}$ Dr.		868 $\frac{1}{3}$ Dr.

When these amounts are subtracted from the sum total of all the interest for
the fourth year, we determine the maximum and minimum amounts for the combined
interest of the first and fourth payments.

6813 $\frac{1}{4}$ Dr.	6813 $\frac{1}{4}$ Dr.
868 $\frac{1}{3}$ Dr.	868 $\frac{1}{2}$ Dr.
Interest on Payments I and IV Max. 5944 $\frac{11}{12}$ Dr.	Min. 5944 $\frac{9}{12}$ Dr.

Since the fourth payment had as interest a maximum of 2000 Dr. and a
minimum of 1600 Dr. the amount of interest for the first payment was:

Maximum   4344 $\frac{11}{12}$ Dr.   or   Minimum   3944 $\frac{9}{12}$ Dr.

Furthermore, since the sum of the amounts of interest on the first and fourth payments must remain constant (within one obol), and since the amount of interest on the fourth payment may vary only by intervals of 20 Dr., the amount of interest on the first payment as well may vary only by intervals of 20 Dr., and possible numbers which can be restored run in the following sequences:

$3944 \frac{9}{12}$ Dr.	or	$3944 \frac{11}{12}$ Dr.
$3964 \frac{9}{12}$ Dr.	or	$3964 \frac{11}{12}$ Dr.
$3984 \frac{9}{12}$ Dr.	or	$3984 \frac{11}{12}$ Dr.
etc.		etc.
$4344 \frac{9}{12}$ Dr.	or	$4344 \frac{11}{12}$ Dr.

Within the given limits of restoration there is only one possibility. Interest must be reckoned on 59 Tal. 4720 Dr. for 355 days. The amount of interest is 4244.85 Dr., which may be written in Greek numerals as XXXXHHΔΔΔΔΗΗΗΗΙΙΙC, occupying, as demanded by the requirements of the stone, a space of 19 letters. A correction must have been made here by the auditors on the amount of interest as reckoned by the table, p. 32. I suggest that the amount of interest was first calculated on 59 Tal. 4750 Dr. and that from the result thus obtained was subtracted the interest which would accumulate on 30 Dr. in 355 days, determined probably by the use of a table similar to that on p. 34. (cf. pp. 36-37).

It is evident now that the tribe Akamantis held the first prytany in the year 423-2, and the spacing of the letters on the stone necessitates that we assume a line of 74 letters and restore the date as the eleventh day of the prytany.

The amount of interest on the fourth payment is given by subtraction as exactly 1700 Dr., and we know that the principal was outstanding for 85 days. The payment was made in the eighth prytany (cf. p. 55), and I have restored the date as the 25th day of the prytany, with a length of line of 74 letters.

After the numeral XΓHH in line 44 are four letter spaces uninscribed. At the beginning of the next line before the word δόσις there was room for the six letters of the word πέμπτε which would normally be restored there. But if πέμπτε is restored in line 45 the last four spaces of line 44 must be left blank. This is not impossible at the end of a line where one rubric is closed and another begins, but the normal practice of our inscription is to leave one, or at most two, blank letter spaces between the records of the several payments within any given year. Perhaps we should restore the word τελευταία in lines 44-45 in place of πέμπτε, leaving only one letter space blank after the numeral ΧℙΗΗ. For a similar variation from the use of ordinal numerals in listing the payments compare the use of hετέρα in place of δευτέρα in line 20. If the restoration which I suggest as probable, though not at all necessary, is correct, the word τελευταία may have been used because of the fact that the fifth payment of the fourth year was actually the last payment to be made from the treasure of Athena Polias during the quadrennium.

The amount of interest to be restored for the second payment is determined by the following considerations, while the only two possibilities of computation are

ΤΤ🅇ℙ	in 281 days yields	Hℙ△ϜϜϜΙΙΙΙ[ΙC]
[Τ]ΤΤ🅇ℙ	in 209 days yields	Hℙ△ϜϜϜΙΙΙΙ[C].

Of these the first alone can be correct, because the second runs for only 209 days and necessitates also an interest period shorter than 209 days for the third payment.

Assuming, then, an interest period of 208 days for the third payment, we may determine the amount of principal as approximately 13 Tal. 5966 Dr. If this amount is substituted in the table of minimum amounts given above on p. 61 we obtain the sum total of principal for the year as follows:

Principal of Payment I	59 Tal.	4720 Dr.	
Principal of Payment II	3 Tal.	5500 Dr.	(the premise here calls for this restoration)
Principal of Payment III	13 Tal.	5966 Dr.	
Principal of Payment IV	100 Tal.	Dr.	
Principal of Payment V	15 Tal.	1812 Dr.	
Total	192 Tal.	5998 Dr.	

This total is larger than that actually preserved on the stone in line 47, and cannot be correct. The restoration of the amount of the second payment, therefore, as [Τ]ΤΤ🅇ℙ with interest computed in 209 days as Hℙ△ϜϜϜΙΙΙΙ[C] will have to be discarded. We may be sure that the figures ΤΤ🅇ℙ actually on the stone give the total amount of the principal, and that interest was computed in 281 days as Hℙ△ϜϜϜΙΙΙΙ[ΙC].

The amounts of interest in the fourth year have now all been determined and may be summarized in the following table:

Payment I	59 Tal.	4720 Dr.	in 355 days yields	$4244\frac{9}{12}$ Dr.
Payment II	2 Tal.	5500 Dr.	in 281 days yields	$163\frac{11}{12}$ Dr.
Payment III	?		in ? days yields	$582\frac{2}{12}$ Dr.
Payment IV	100 Tal.		in 85 days yields	1700 Dr.
Payment V	?		in ? days yields	$122\frac{5}{12}$ Dr.

Total interest for the fourth year (c/. line 48) $6813\frac{1}{4}$ Dr.

The amounts of principal for the third and fifth payments must be such that the total sum of the five payments shall equal 192 Tal. $1642\frac{5}{12}$ Dr. (line 47), and such that the amounts expressed in Greek numerical signs shall fulfill the physical requirements of the stone for restoration. At the same time the dates of the separate payments must take their place in a comprehensible scheme of the Athenian calendar.

I submit the following figures which give, I believe, the only restorations possible.

For the third payment interest is computed on 11 Tal. 3300 Dr. for 252 days as $582\frac{1}{6}$ Dr. Lines 41-43 should be restored in part [τρίτε δόσι]ς [ἐπὶ τὲς . . . .⁶ . . . ίδος πρυτανείας τετά]ρτες πρυτανευόσες τετάρτει τὲς πρυτα[νείας πρὸς] Σαμ[ίος ⳨ΤΧΧΧΗΗΗ τόκος τούτοις ἐγένετο] ⳨⳨𐅅ΔΔⱵⱵΙ.

The restoration demands a line of 74 letters. I have followed Unger's conjecture in reading [πρὸς] Σαμ[ίος], and it may be observed that the words do fill the required space on the stone.

For the fifth payment interest is computed on 18 Tal. $122\frac{5}{12}$ Dr. for 34 days as $122\frac{5}{12}$ Dr. Lines 44-46 should be restored in part as [τελευταία δόσις ἐπὶ τὲς Λεοντίδο]ς πρυτανείας δεκάτες πρυτανευόσες τ[ὲι τρίτ]ει τὲς πρ[υτανείας ⳨⳨ΤΤΤΗⱵⱵⱵΙΙⅭ τόκος τούτον] ΗⱵⱵⱵΙΙⅭ.

Line 44 contains 74 letters, as do the lines immediately preceding, and line 45 contains 75 letters, as does also the line immediately following. The numeral for the date τ[ὲι τρίτ]ει is unusual, because the article is elsewhere omitted. But here no normal restoration is possible, because there are 6 letter spaces to be filled between the *tau* of frg. *b* and the *epsilon* of frg. *c*. The word τριακοστὲι is too long by one letter — and impossible for other reasons as well — and the word τετάρτει is too short by one letter. The words τὲι τρίτει fill the requirements of the space exactly, and are in fact necessary for the mathematical calculations. The last prytany is known to have contained 36 days (c/. p. 16) and in order that the last payment may have been outstanding for 34 days it is necessary to assume that it was made on the 3ʳᵈ day of the prytany.

9

Now that we know of divergences from the customary formulae of the year in the record of this last payment (the probable use of the word τελευταία instead of πέμπτε to give the number of the payment, and certainly the use of the article with the date) it is less surprising to find also the older phrase τόκος τούτον in place of the usual τόκος τούτοις ἐγένετο.

The interest as I have given it may be reckoned according to the table on p. 32.

Third Payment: 11 Tal. 3300 Dr. in 252 days

10 Tal.	in one day yields 2 Dr.	
	in 252 days yields	504 Dr.
1 Tal. 2750 Dr.	in one day yields $1\frac{3}{4}$ obols	
	in 252 days yields 441 obols	$=$ 73 Dr. 3 obols
550 Dr.	in one day yields $\frac{550}{1250} \times \frac{1}{4}$ obol	
	$= \frac{1}{9}$ obol (approximately)	
	in 252 days yields 28 obols	$=$ 4 Dr. 4 obols

11 Tal. 3300 Dr. in 252 days yields   582 Dr. 1 obol

Fifth Payment: 18 Tal. $122\frac{5}{12}$ Dr. in 34 days

15 Tal.	in one day yields 3 Dr.	
	in 34 days yields	102 Dr.
3 Tal. $122\frac{5}{12}$ Dr.	in one day yields $3\frac{1}{2} + \frac{1}{8}$ obol	
	in 34 days yields $3\frac{5}{8} \times 34$	
	$= 102 + 20\frac{5}{8}$ obol (approximately)	
	$= 122\frac{1}{2}$ obols (approximately)	$=$ 20 Dr. $2\frac{1}{2}$ obols

18 Tal. $122\frac{5}{12}$ Dr. in 34 days yields   122 Dr. $2\frac{1}{2}$ obols

This last reckoning is not mathematically exact, but we have seen that accuracy, as we understand the term, is not in every instance possible (p. 37). And I have found no combination of amounts of principal for the third and fifth payments (the sum of which must equal 29 Tal. $3422\frac{5}{12}$ Dr.) which gives a more satisfactory reckoning of interest than that proposed above. Perhaps we have to deal with a case of parablepsis on the part of the scribe, for it may be more than a coincidence that both the sums of principal and of interest end in the figures -ΗΔΔⱵⱵΙΙC.

The dates which are now restored for the various payments of the fourth year again indicate a calendar with prytanies of 36 and 37 days.

Senatorial Year 423-2 (containing 365 days)

No. of Prytany	Days in Prytany	No. of days before end of quadrennium	Dates of Payments
I	*37 days	(365-329)	First payment made on the 11th day (355)
II	*37 days	(328-292)	
III	*36 days	(291-256)	Second Payment made on the 11th day (281)
IV	37 days	(255-219)	Third payment made on the 4th day (252)
V	37 days	(218-182)	
VI	36 days	(181-146)	
VII	36 days	(145-110)	
VIII	37 days	(109- 73)	Fourth payment made on the 25th day (85)
IX	36 days	(72- 37)	
X	*36 days	(36- 1)	Fifth payment made on the 3rd day (34)

We have left until the last a detailed discussion of the restorations in the record of the first year, for although the evidence is more nearly complete than that of any of the other years the problem of restoration presents some peculiar difficulties. On the other hand, we have in the course of our argument so far made several determinations of numerals and dates in the record of payments of the first year. We may give the following summary of what we know from the stone or of what has been proved so far:

	Principal	Interest		No. of days	Date and Prytany
Payment I	20 Tal.	5696 (cf. p. 26)	Dr.	1424	Pryt. II, 4
Payment II	50 Tal.	2 Tal. 1970	Dr.	1397	Pryt. II, 31
Payment III	?	1 Tal. 1719$\frac{1}{3}$	Dr.	?	Pryt. IV, 5
Payment IV	44 Tal. 3000 Dr. (cf. p. 36)	1 Tal. 4701$\frac{1}{6}$ (cf. p. 35)	Dr.	1202 (cf. p. 36)	Pryt. VIII, 5
Payment V	100 Tal.	3 Tal. 5940	Dr.	1197	Pryt. VIII, 10 (cf. p. 36)
Payment VI	?	4172$\frac{2}{3}$ (cf. p. 35)	Dr.	?	Pryt. X, 7

Total Principal 261 Tal. 5610$\frac{7}{12}$ Dr.   (ΗΗΡΔΤΡΡΗ[ΔΙΙΙϹ])   (cf. p. 47)

Total Interest   11 Tal. 199$\frac{1}{6}$ Dr.   ([ΔΤΗ]ΡΔΔΔΔΠΗΗΗΙ)   (cf. pp. 31 and 35)

* The asterisk marks those prytanies where the number of days is certain. Some interchange is possible among the others, though the sequence of 36 and 37 day prytanies is fixed throughout the year in such a way that the total number of days is 365.

We have observed that the payments made in the second, third, and fourth years of the quadrennium give a calendar year with prytanies of 36 and 37 days. The same is true of the payments listed in the above table for the first year, where the number of days for which interest was reckoned is known.

Even without the evidence from the third and sixth payments we are now justified in considering this calendar system established, and it gives us material assistance in determining the amounts of principal for these two payments as yet unknown.

For example, since the fifth payment was made on the 10th day of the eighth prytany and since interest was reckoned for 1197 days, we may conclude that the date of the sixth payment (Pryt. X, 7) represents an interest period of 1128 days (if the eighth and ninth prytanies contained 36 days each), or 1126 days (if the eighth and ninth prytanies contained 37 days each), or possibly 1127 days (if one of these two prytanies contained 36 and the other 37 days).

The amount of interest accrued on the sixth payment in 1126 days represents a principal of approximately 18 Tal. 3172 Dr. (computed by decimal notation), and in 1128 days it represents a principal of approximately 18 Tal. 2975 Dr. (computed in the same way). But the physical requirements of the stone compel us to restore the principal as exactly 18 Tal. 3000 Dr., for this numeral alone can be accommodated in the space available in line 13.

Interest on 18 Tal. 3000 Dr. in 1128 days should be reckoned as follows:

15 Tal.		in one day yields 3 Dr.	
		in 1128 days yields 3×1128	3384 Dr.
3 Tal.	2000 Dr.	in one day yields 4 obols	
		in 1128 days yields 4512 obols	$=$ 752 Dr.
	1000 Dr.	in one day yields $\frac{1000}{1250} \times \frac{1}{4} = \frac{1}{5}$ obol	
		$= \frac{1}{9} + \frac{1}{12}$ obol	
		in 1128 days yields	
		$126 + 94 = 220$ obols	$=$ 36 Dr. 4 obols.
18 Tal.	3000 Dr.	in 1128 days yields	4172 Dr. 4 obols.

This amount, expressed in Greek numerical signs, is XXXXHℙΔΔⱵⱵIIII, and is in fact the numeral which we have restored as interest on the sixth payment.

The amount of the third payment may now be determined by adding together the amounts of the 1st, 2nd, 4th, 5th, and 6th payments, and subtracting the result from the sum total of all six payments. The principal of the third payment amounts to 28 Tal. 5610 $\frac{7}{12}$ Dr. This figure is expressed in Greek numerical signs as ΔΔΓΤΤΤⱵⱵⱵΗΔΙΙΙC and I have restored it in Plates I and II in line 8. It may be observed that it conforms perfectly to the *stoichedon* arrangement of the letters on the stone and occupies the amount of space available for the restoration.

The amount of the interest on this principal is preserved on the stone in line 9 as ΤΧⱵΗΗΔΠⱵⱵⱵΙΙ, and an arithmetical computation shows that with the amounts of principal and interest here given the payment was outstanding approximately 1334 days. It is further known that the payment was made on the fifth day of the 4th prytany (426-5).

In the discussion of the calendar system which we have been developing from the study of this inscription I have left this item till the last because it presents an obvious anomaly. We expect the fifth day of the 4th prytany to fall 1349 or 1350 days before the terminus to which interest was reckoned, since the official year was made up of prytanies of 36 and 37 days each. We find here that a mathematical computation places the day in question 1334 days before that terminus. I feel certain that this cannot be correct, if for no other reason than that it necessitates the assumption that the third prytany contained approximately 52 days! — and the further assumption that the fourth, fifth, sixth, and seventh prytanies contained approximately 33 days each!! The variation is too great to be explained by any calendar system. I have made the attempt to remedy this discrepancy by different restorations of the amount of principal for the third payment, but since the sum total of principal for the year is fixed, within very narrow limits, by the reading on the stone itself, we are obliged to add to the amount of the sixth payment whatever thousands of drachmae may be subtracted from the third payment, and again the same anomaly arises in a different quarter. We find that the eighth and ninth prytanies of 426-5 are extraordinarily long and that the following four prytanies are correspondingly short. There is, in fact, no way of avoiding the anomaly if we maintain that the amount of interest given in line 9 is correct.

I was for a long time unwilling to believe that the correctness of this amount should be questioned, for we have every reason, *a priori,* to expect accuracy in the official audit of state accounts. But we have discovered already one mistake (pp. 48-50) where the numeral Ⱶ was written in place of Ⱶ in the figure preserved in line 112, and we have seen that this was an error not of the stonecutter but of the auditors themselves, for it is involved in the subsequent reckonings. We have also demonstrated that every entry of Athena's accounts, with the exception of the third payment of the first year, indicates a calendar system with prytanies of 36 and 37 days.

I make, therefore, the suggestion that the amount of interest on the third payment in 426-5 is incorrectly given, and that the mistake is due to a false copying of the amount of the principal when the computation was being made. The interest recorded on the stone is such as would accrue in 1349 days on a principal of 28 Tal. 3610 Dr. Since two of the items of this year contain the figures for 3000 Dr., it is perhaps a simple case of parablepsis that the computer from his copy read 3000 Dr. here, instead of the proper 5000 Dr. (which was later copied correctly into the record), although the other figures in this numeral, talents, hundreds of drachmae, etc., were copied correctly.

Interest on 28 Tal. 3610+ Dr. in 1349 days should be reckoned as follows (cf. table p. 32).

25 Tal.		in one day yields 5 Dr.	
		in 1349 days yields 5×1349 $= 6745$ Dr.	
3 Tal.	3250 Dr.	in one day yields $4\frac{1}{4}$ obols	
		in 1349 days yields $5733\frac{1}{4}$ obols $= 955\frac{1}{2}+$ Dr.	
	360 Dr.	in one day yields $\frac{360}{1250} \times \frac{1}{4} = \frac{9}{125} = \frac{1}{12}$ ob.	
		(a nearer approximation in one fraction is impossible cf. p. 33)	
		in 1349 days yields $112\frac{5}{12}$ obols $= 18\frac{5}{6}$ Dr.	

28 Tal. 3610 Dr. in 1349 days yields   7719   Dr. 2 obols

We may now illustrate in tabular form the senatorial years and lengths of prytany as they have been determined in our study so far:

Year 426-5   contains 366 days   (1464-1099)

Pryt.	I	37 days	(1464-1428)	
Pryt.	II	37 days	(1427-1391)	First payment made on 4th day (1424)
				Second payment made on 31st day (1397)
Pryt.	III	37 days	(1390-1354)	
Pryt.	IV	37 days	(1353-1317)	Third payment made on 5th day (1349)
Pryt.	V	37 days	(1316-1280)	
Pryt.	VI	37 days	(1279-1243)	
Pryt.	VII	36 days	(1242-1207)	
Pryt.	VIII	36 days	(1206-1171)	Fourth payment made on 5th day (1202)
				Fifth payment made on 10th day (1197)
Pryt.	IX	36 days	(1170-1135)	
Pryt.	X	36 days	(1134-1099)	Sixth payment made on 7th day (1128)

Year 425-4   contains 368 days   (1098-731)

Pryt.	I	37 days	(1098-1062)
Pryt.	II	37 days	(1061-1025)

Year 425-4   contains 368 days   (1098-731)

Pryt. III   37 days   (1024-988)

Pryt. IV   37 days   (987-951)   First payment made on 3rd day (985)

Pryt. V   37 days   (950-914)

Pryt. VI   37 days   (913-877)

Pryt. VII   37 days   (876-840)

Pryt. VIII   37 days   (839-803)

Pryt. IX   36 days   (802-767)   Second payment made on 15th day (788)

Pryt. X   36 days   (766-731)

Year 424-3   contains 365 days   (730-366)

Pryt. I   37 days   (730-694)   First payment made on 26th day (705)

Pryt. II   37 days   (693-657)

Pryt. III   37 days   (656-620)   Second payment made on 12th day (645)

Pryt. IV   36 days   (619-584)

Pryt. V   36 days   (583-548)

Pryt. VI   36 days   (547-512)

Pryt. VII   37 days   (511-475)   Third payment made on 2nd day (510)

Pryt. VIII   37 days   (474-438)   Fourth payment made on 30th day (445)

Pryt. IX   36 days   (437-402)

Pryt. X   36 days   (401-366)

Year 423-2   contains 365 days   (365-1)

Pryt. I   37 days   (365-329)   First payment made on 11th day (355)

Pryt. II   37 days   (328-292)

Pryt. III   36 days   (291-256)   Second payment made on 11th day (281)

Pryt. IV   37 days   (255-219)   Third payment made on 4th day (252)

Pryt. V   37 days   (218-182)

Pryt. VI   36 days   (181-146)

Pryt. VII   36 days   (145-110)

Pryt. VIII   37 days   (109- 73)   Fourth payment made on 25th day (85)

Pryt. IX   36 days   (72- 37)

Pryt. X   36 days   (36- 1)   Fifth payment made on 3rd day (34)

The total number of days in the quadrennium from Pryt. I, 1 (426-5) to Pryt. X, 36 (423-2) is 1464.

It is evident from the above tables that although the prytanies contain regularly 36 or 37 days there is no definite order of precedence or alternation. We observe also that the senatorial calendar of the Athenians in the fifth century was established on a basis very closely approximating our own solar year, and that the years of the senatorial calendar were free from intercalation. We shall return later to a study of the relation between the senatorial and civil calendars. At present it is sufficient to notice that the complete revision of the political machinery of Athens in the time of Kleisthenes was accompanied by just as drastic a revision of the official calendar. The older civil calendar continued, of course, side by side with the new, sanctioned by religious observance, but the new calendar of ten prytanies in each year, free from cycles and intercalations, was an achievement in simplicity worthy of the name of the great statesman. Kleisthenes realized the advantages of a calendar regulated by the solar year and we must concede him the honor of having introduced such a calendar scheme into the official life of Ancient Athens.

CHAPTER VII

ATHENA NIKE AND THE OTHER GODS

We have now completed the restoration, except for some minor details, of that part of the inscription which gives the record of money borrowed from Athena Polias during the quadrennium from 426-5 to 423-2. In lines 51-53 we find the record of the only loan made by Athena Nike during this four year period. The amount of the principal must be restored as six talents (*cf.* p. 49), but we have as yet made no attempt to determine the date on which the payment was made.

The space available for the number of the prytany is sufficient for eight letters, five at the end of line 51 and three at the beginning of line 52. The possibilities are δευτέρας, τετάρτες, and hεβδόμες. On the other hand the space which we find available for the name of the prytanizing tribe in line 51 amounts to eleven letters, and the two tribal names which in the genitive case have eleven letters are 'Ακαμαντίδος and Πανδιονίδος. We have found, however, in our restoration of the accounts of Athena Polias in this year that Akamantis held the first prytany, and that Pandionis held the third prytany, so that neither of these names can be restored here if the number of the prytany is 2nd, 4th, or 7th. If we restore either Akamantis or Pandionis as the name of the prytany, then the number of the prytany must be restored as πρότες or τρίτες, either of which possibilities is too short by two letters. If we restore the numeral correctly we must place a word of ten letters instead of eleven in line 51 as the name of the prytany. This latter solution seems to me correct, especially since it makes possible the restoration of the date as the fourth day of the fourth prytany, when we know that a loan was made also from the treasure of Athena Polias. The name of the prytanizing tribe in the fourth prytany contained, in the genitive case, ten letters (*cf.* line 42) and I assume that this same name was written in line 51 (spaced so that it occupied eleven letter spaces on the stone) and that payments were made on the same day both from the treasures of Athena Polias and Athena Nike. The fourth day of the fourth prytany allows the reckoning of interest for 252 days, and I have given the tentative restoration of the interest on 6 Tal. as 302 Dr. 1 obol.

The calculation is as follows:

5 Tal.	in one day yields 1 Dr.	
	in 252 days yields	252 Dr.
5000 Dr.	in one day yields 1 obol	
	in 252 days yields 252 obols	42 Dr.
1000 Dr.	in one day yields $\frac{1000}{1250} \times \frac{1}{4} = \frac{1}{5}$ obol	
	$= \frac{1}{9} + \frac{1}{12}$ obol (*cf.* also p. 59)	
	in 252 days yields $28 + 21 = 49$ obols —	8 Dr. 1 obol

6 Tal.	in 252 days yields	302 Dr. 1 obol

Following the record of this item borrowed from Athena Nike there was cut on the stone (lines 54-97) the record of payments made from the treasury of the Other Gods. There were only two payments and both of these fell in the year 423-2. In the case of each payment the date is given not only by the senatorial calendar, but by the civil calendar as well; the component parts of each payment, as contributed by the individual sanctuaries, are given in detail with interest reckoned on each amount of principal; for each payment there is a summary giving the total amount of principal and the total amount of interest; and in conclusion there is given the sum total of the principal of both payments, followed by the sum total of the interest accrued on both payments.

We have already discussed the date of the second payment (Pryt. X, 20=Skir. 23), but the date of the first payment has remained undetermined. We must now see what evidence exists for the fixing of this date.

We called attention above (p. 14) to the fact that in line 76 of the inscription there are seven spaces for numerals between the words ἐπὶ Γοργοίνο ἄρχοντος and the preserved figures on frg. *e* (ḤHⱭ). The word Γοργοίνο begins from the left margin of the stone in line 76, as may be seen in Plate I, and the restoration of the phrase τ̑ες πρότες δόσεος ἐπὶ Γοργοίνο ἄρχοντος in lines 75-76 necessitates leaving a space of three letters uninscribed at the end of line 75. This could be remedied by writing τ̑ες πρότες δόσεος τ̑ες ἐπὶ Γοργοίνο ἄρχοντος although the repetition of the word τ̑ες is unusual. The spacing of letters at the end of line 75 might also be made satisfactory by changing the formula ἐπὶ Γοργοίνο ἄρχοντος to read ἐπὶ τὲς Γοργοίνο ἀρχὲς. If this reading is adopted we should have to restore the numeral in line 76 as [. . .⁶. . . ⋈ΓΗΗ]ḤΗΓ[ΔΔΔΔ], but we shall soon see that this reading of the numeral is impossible. Besides, the phrase ἐπὶ τὲς Γοργοίνο ἀρχὲς is paralleled in this inscription only by the expanded form ἐπὶ τὲς Γοργοίνο ἀρχὲς καὶ χσυναρχόντον. In my restoration I have kept the words ἐπὶ Γοργοίνο ἄρχοντος, as they are found also in line 94, and have satisfied the requirements of spacing at the end of line 75 by restoring τὲς πρότες δόσεος τὲς ἐπὶ Γοργοίνο ἄρχοντος.

In the record of the second payment it was very easy to determine that interest had been reckoned for 17 days, and this computation was possible not only with the sums total of principal and interest, but also with several of the individual amounts of principal and interest. In the record of the first payment, unfortunately, the stone is so broken that for no single loan are the amounts of principal and interest both preserved. Only the sum total of interest is preserved, in line 76, as XXHΔΔ − −, and the sum total of the principal may be restored as [. .³. . ⋈ΓΗΗ]ḤΗΓ[ΔΔΔΔ] (*cf.* pp. 14-15). With the restoration ἐπὶ τὲς Γοργοίνο ἀρχὲς in lines 75-76 the sum total of the principal may be restored as [. . .⁶. . . ⋈ΓΗΗ]ḤΗΓ[ΔΔΔΔ]. We shall return to these possibilities later, when we find the evidence for choosing between them.

In line 57 the name of the prytanizing tribe is either Akamantis or Pandionis, and the number of the prytany is consequently either first or third. We may eliminate Pandionis in the third prytany, however, because the interest on a loan made in the third prytany must have been reckoned over a period of time between 291 and 256 days (*cf.* table p. 71). And we are able to prove that the period of interest accumulation was greater than 291 days.

Suppose, for example, that interest was reckoned on the payment of 86 Dr. from the treasure of Adrasteia (line 67) for 291 days. The amount of the interest would be five obols (ΙΙΙΙΙ), but there is not room on the stone for the restoration of this figure which, in Greek characters, would occupy three letter spaces. The end of line 67 and the beginning of line 68 must be restored as follows:

['Αδρασ]τείας ΓΔΔΔΓⱵ τό[κος τούτο . | Βενδ]ίδος etc.

I consider the restoration [Βενδ]ῖδος at the beginning of line 68 as practically certain. Adrasteia and Bendis are known to have been associated (*cf. I.G.* I², 310, lines 207-208) and in the passage in question here the amount of money from the common treasury has been credited equally to them, 86 Dr. to Adrasteia and 86 Dr. to Bendis. Only one letter space is left at the end of line 67 for the numeral representing the interest accrued on the loan from Adrasteia. The amount to be

restored cannot have been |||||, which occupies three letter spaces, but must have
been ⊦, occupying only one letter space. This is true whether we adhere to the
restoration [Βενδ]ῖδος for line 68, or restore in its place the form [Θέμ]ιδος, which is
shorter by one letter. Now it is possible to reckon the number of days on which
interest of one drachma would have accrued on a principal of 86 Dr. as approximately
340 or 350, and this falls well within the limits of the first prytany (cf. table p. 71)
so that lines 57-58 may be restored

[- -- ἐπὶ τῆς ᾽Ακαμαντ]ίδ[ος πρυτανείας πρότες
πρυτανευόσες ἑκατομβαιō]νος ὀγ[δόει --   ].

It is certain that 423-2 was an ordinary year (cf. pp. 86-92 below) and the
name of the month to be restored is Hekatombaeon, rather than Metageitnion, which
would have been necessary for an intercalary year. We know also from line 79 of
this inscription that the 23rd of Skirophorion coincided with the 20th day of the tenth
prytany, and that it fell 17 days before the terminus to which interest was reckoned.
Between Σκιροφοριōνος ὀγδόε φθίνοντος and the previous ἑκατομβαιōνος ὀγδόε
φθίνοντος there were 325 days, if Hekatombaeon was hollow and Skirophorion full,
or 324 days, if Hekatombaeon was full and Skirophorion hollow. The date ἑκατομβαιōνος ὀγδόε φθίνοντος fell, therefore, 342 or 341 days before the terminus to which
interest was reckoned. The number of days corresponds exactly with the possible
340 or 350 which we determined above on the basis of the interest rate on the
payment of 86 Dr. from the treasure of Adrasteia, and indicates the restoration of the
date in line 58 as

[ἑκατομβαιō]νος ὀγ[δόει φθίνοντος   ].

With the knowledge now at our disposal that the payment was outstanding
341 or 342 days we may determine exactly the amount of the principal on the entire
first payment (line 76). The figure must be restored as [ΔΔΔ⋈⊓ΗΗ]ΗΗ⋈[ΔΔΔΔ], which
in 342 days yields 2120 Dr. 1 obol. The amount may be reckoned as follows:

30 Tal.	in one day yields 6 Dr.	
	in 342 days yields 6 × 342	= 2052 Dr.
5000 Dr.	in one day yields 1 obol	
	in 342 days yields 342 obols	= 57 Dr.
1000 Dr.	in one day yields $\frac{1000}{1250}×\frac{1}{4}=\frac{1}{5}=\frac{1}{9}+\frac{1}{12}$ob.	
	in 342 days yields 67 obols (approximately)	11 Dr. 1 obol

31 Tal. (or 30 Tal. 5990 Dr.) in 342 days yields   2120 Dr. 1 obol.

This amount of interest agrees with that preserved on the stone in line 76. If interest is computed for 341 days the amount is too small, and this possible number must be rejected. As a direct consequence we may be certain that in the year 423-2 the month Hekatombaeon was hollow, not full, and that the sequence of days in the months of the year was as follows:

Hekatombaeon	29
Metageitnion	30
Boedromion	29
Pyanepsion	30
Maimakterion	29
Posideion	30
Gamelion	29
Anthesterion	30
Elaphebolion	29
Munichion	30
Thargelion	29
Skirophorion	30
Total Civil Year	354

With the longer restoration of the amount of principal in line 76, [. . ."̣. . . ⋈ΓΗΗ]ḤΗ⋈[ΔΔΔΔ], any determination of the interest as it is preserved on the stone is mathematically impossible, and this longer restoration must be rejected (cf. p. 75 above). As a direct consequence of this observation we may be sure that the phrase ἐπὶ Γοργοίνο ἄρχοντος in lines 75-76 is properly restored, whatever may be the irregularity in the demonstrative use of the word τῆς at the end of line 75.

The total principal of the first payment made from the treasure of the Other Gods may now be added to the total principal of the second payment to give the sum total in line 96:

[ΔΔΔ⋈ΓΗΗ]ḤΗ⋈[ΔΔΔΔ]   line 76
ΔΔΤΤΤ⋈ΓΗΗΗΗ[⋈ΔΔΔΔΓⱵⱵⱵ]   lines 94-95
[⋈ΤΤ]ΤΤ⋈[ΓΗΗΗΗ]⋈ΔΔΔΓⱵⱵⱵ   line 96

I have restored lines 95-96 in part as follows:

κεφάλαιον ἀναλόματος τὸ ἀ[ρχαίο|ἐπὶ Γοργοίνο ἄρχοντος ᵛ ⋈ΤΤ]ΤΤ⋈[ΓΗΗΗΗ]⋈ΔΔΔΓⱵⱵⱵ.

A blank space is left before the numeral, as well as after, and the figures are spaced somewhat more widely than in a *stoichedon* arrangement of the letters. Both of these divergences are amply justified by the spacing of the figures in the numeral of line 94 (*cf.* Plate I), and we have already seen that the figures ⌐HHHH, which must be restored in the center of the numeral, occupy a space of seven letters intead of a space of five (*cf.* p. 15).

It is impossible to restore exactly the amount of interest on the first payment made from the treasure of the Other Gods, because it was actually computed not on the sum total of the principal as a loan outstanding for 342 days, but it was reckoned by adding together the several amounts of interest accrued on the individual payments of the separate sanctuaries. These small amounts of interest were often of necessity approximated to the nearest obol or fraction of an obol, and the margin of error, probably in favor of the lender, increases as the several items are added together. The figure actually on the stone, therefore, was slightly higher than 2120 Dr. 1 obol, which sum was determined by the calculation on p. 76 above, but probably less than 2121 Dr. Since it is impossible to be exact I have left the numeral unrestored at the end of line 76, and have indicated the sum total of the interest in line 97 merely as 2120+82=2202 Dr.

We may now return to the problem of the restoration of the date of the first payment. The loan was made in the prytany of Akamantis, the first prytany of the year, and on the 22nd day of the month Hekatombaeon. This was 342 days before the terminus to which interest was reckoned and consequently on the 24th day of the first prytany (*cf.* table p. 71). We may restore lines 57-59 as follows:

[ἐπὶ τές βολές ἧι Δεμέτρι]ος πρότ[ος ἐγραμμάτευε ἐπὶ τές Ἀκαμαντ]ίδ[ος πρυτανείας πρότες πρυτανευόσες hεκατομβαιό]νος ὀγ[δόει φθίνοντος τετάρτει καὶ εἰκοστέι τές πρυτανείας   ].

The date here is given in full

1. by the secretary of the senate.
2. by the name and sequence of the prytanizing tribe.
3. by the day of the civil month.
4. by the day of the prytany.

Between the last words of this date and the beginning of the list of sanctuaries which participated in the payment is a *lacuna* of 13 letter spaces, which is exactly suited to the restoration of the words τάδε παρέδοσαν. I have suggested above (p. 8) in a provisional restoration of lines 54-56, and following the reading as it is given in the *Corpus,* that the words τάδε παρέδοσαν appeared in line 55 in the phrase τάδε παρέδοσαν hοι ταμίαι τόν ἄλλον θεόν, etc. I believe, however, that in line 55 a relative

pronoun must be substituted in place of the word τάδε, since the paragraph which
begins with line 54 and continues to line 59 cannot be interpreted when τάδε
παρέδοσαν appears both in line 55 and in line 59. I suggest that the relative ηόσα
should be substituted in place of τάδε in line 55 and that the whole preamble should
be considered as falling into two distinct sentences.

The first sentence reads as follows:

τάδε ἐλογίσαντο ηοι λογισταὶ ὀφελόμενα τοῖς ἄλλοις θεοῖς ἐν τοῖς τέτταρσιν ἔτεσιν ἐκ
Παναθεναίον ἐς Παναθέναια ηόσα παρέδοσαν ηοι ταμίαι τὸν ἄλλον θεὸν Γόργοινος
Οἰνείδο Ἰκαριεὺς καὶ χσυνάρχοντες ἐκ τὸν ἑκάστο χρεμάτον ηελλενοταμίαις καὶ
στρατεγοῖς . .⁴. . καὶ χσυνάρχοσιν.

This sentence explains the nature of the two entries which are to follow,
and is followed by the second sentence giving the date and introducing the amounts
of principal and interest:

ἐπὶ τῆς βολῆς ηῆι Δεμέτριος πρῶτος ἐγραμμάτευε ἐπὶ τῆς Ἀκαμαντίδος πρυτανείας
πρότες πρυτανευόσες ηεκατομβαιῶνος ὀγδόει φθίνοντος τετάρτει καὶ εἰκοστῆι τῆς
πρυτανείας τάδε παρέδοσαν Ἀρτέμιδος Ἀγροτέρας   etc.

The two payments from the treasury of the Other Gods were made in the
year 423-2 and the amounts were given to the hellenotamiae and the generals. The
restoration [ηελλενοταμίαις καὶ στρατ]εγοῖ[ς] in line 56 is certain (cf. Kirchner's note
on lines 2-3 of I.G. I², 324 in the Corpus, Vol. I, editio minor, p. 153). This same
restoration should be made also in lines 37-38, and since these lines give the
disposition of Athena's payments in the same year, we may be certain that the board
of generals was the same.[1] In line 38 we have the demotic of the name of the general
given (Μυρρινοσίοι) and between the words ηελλενοταμίαις καὶ στρατεγοῖς and this
demotic there is only room for a word of four letters, which must have been the name
of the general, in the dative case. This same name of four letters must be restored at
the end of line 56 followed by the words καὶ χσυνάρχοσιν. The demotic of the general's
name was omitted in the record of payments from the Other Gods, just as the demotic
of the name of the secretary of the senate was omitted in line 57 (cf. Plate I).

This is another indication that the preamble for the record of payments from
the treasure of the Other Gods should be separated into two distinct rubrics with
restorations as suggested above.

In general, I have not attempted restorations of the individual amounts of
principal and interest in the two payments. We may be certain, of course, that the

[1] We know that the boards of hellenotamiae were different, for one payment was made before the
Panathenaic festival of 423-2 and the other payment after the festival. Cf. pp. 17-19 above.

interest on the 86 Dr. contributed by Bendis (line 68) amounted to one drachma, just as the interest on the 86 Dr. from the treasure of Adrasteia amounted to one drachma (line 67 above). The amount of principal advanced from the moneys of Herakles in Kynosarges (lines 69-70) may also be restored with reasonable certainty as 20 Dr. Some restorations in the record of the second payment are possible, but the exact figure cannot always be determined, and I have left most of the items unrestored.

CHAPTER VIII

CONCLUDING LINES OF THE INSCRIPTION

On pp. 34 and 47 above we have referred to the restoration of lines 98-100 and the numeral there expressed in words has been read as 4001 Tal. 4522 Dr. My restoration is the same as that given in the *editio minor* of the *Corpus*, except that I have restored also the word [τετρακισχιλίαι]ς in line 100.

This restoration I consider certain, because of the limitations of space and the *stoichedon* arrangement of the letters, and I had in fact reached this conclusion before completing the calculations which involve the sums total of money borrowed from Athena Polias expressed in lines 49 and 114. The restoration is, I believe, mathematically as well as epigraphically unique.

The amount of interest which accrued on this sum in 1464 days may be reckoned by the use of the table on p. 32 as follows:

4000 Tal.	in one day yields 800 Dr.	
	in 1464 days yields	1171200 Dr.
1 Tal. 4000 Dr.	in one day yields $\frac{1}{3}$ Dr.	
	in 1464 days yields	488 Dr.
522 Dr.	in one day yields $\frac{522}{1250} \times \frac{1}{4}$ obols	
	$= \frac{1}{9}$ obol approximately	
	in 1464 days yields $162\frac{2}{3}$ obols $=$	27 Dr. $\frac{3}{4}$ obol

4001 Tal. 4522 Dr.	in 1464 days yields	1171715 Dr. $\frac{3}{4}$ obol
	$= 195$ Tal.	1715 Dr. $\frac{3}{4}$ obol

This amount should be written in Greek numerical characters as

HᴲΔΔΔᴨXᴨHHΔᴨC), for which there is ample room on the stone at the beginning of line 101.

The text of lines 102-105 has been given as by Kubicki. The restoration is certain and needs no further comment. The restoration of lines 106-108 has already been discussed (cf. pp. 48 ff.).

The restorations which I have offered for lines 109-123 have no claim to certainty except as regards the numerals in lines 114-116. The general sense of the lines is clear, however, as follows:

Lines 109-111: These lines contain the record of moneys borrowed from Hermes during the previous seven years, with the computation of interest accumulated during the quadrennium from 426-5 to 423-2. There was apparently no loan made by Hermes to the State during the current four year period. The opening words of line 109 are conjectural. The regular formula would be

τάδε ἐλογίσαντο τοῖς hερμõ ἐν τοῖς τέτταρσιν ἔτεσιν hὰ hοι πρότεροι λογισταὶ λελο-γισμένα παρέδοσαν ἐν τοῖς hεπτὰ ἔτεσιν   etc.

I have followed the *stoichedon* arrangement of letters in the restoration of the latter part of this formula, although the *pi* of hεπτά falls at a point on the stone where the letter preserved seems to have been a *tau*. Perhaps the letter is imperfect. I have no alternative to suggest, except that the letters may have been crowded before the *tau,* which is perhaps the *tau* of hεπτά, and more widely spaced after the *tau.*

Line 112: The amount here given is the sum total of borrowings from Athena Nike.

Line 113: This line records the interest due to Athena Nike.

Line 114: This line gives the sum total of principal borrowed from Athena Polias. I regard the words τὸ ἀρχαῖον as neuter accusative singular, not as an erroneous spelling of the genitive plural τõ(ν) ἀρχαίον, as in the *Corpus.*

Line 115: This line gives the total of interest due to Athena Polias.

Line 116: The sum total of the borrowings from Athena Nike and Athena Polias from 433-2 to 423-2.

Line 117: The sum total of the interest due to both Athena Nike and Athena Polias.

Line 118: uninscribed.

Line 119: The total principal borrowed from the Other Gods.

Line 120: The total interest due to the Other Gods.

Line 121: uninscribed.

Line 122: The grand sum total of all moneys borrowed for state expenses during the eleven years from 433-2 to 423-2.

Line 123: The grand sum total of all the interest accrued on the borrowed moneys during the eleven years.

Fragment *h,* which contains parts of lines 108-123, has been represented in Plate I somewhat differently from its publication in the *Corpus Inscriptionum Atticarum.* In particular, the restoration of lines 110 ff. is more satisfactory when the left margin of the fragment throughout these lines is set out only one letter space, instead of two, to the left of the margin determined by lines 108-109 above. Dodwell, in his original reading of the fragment,[1] records the letters ΕΝΔΕΚΑΕΤΕΣ in line 112, while the *sigma* of the word ἔτεσιν is in part actually preserved on the stone today in frg. *f.* The fact that this letter has been recorded on both fragments has caused difficulty to editors of the document, and yet the stone is broken in such a way that part of the letter may have appeared on each fragment. This I assume to have been the case, and frgs. *f* and *h* are probably to be joined approximately as shown in Plate I.

---

[1] Tour through Greece, Vol. I, p. 372.

CHAPTER IX

THE ATHENIAN CALENDAR FROM 434 TO 401 B.C.

PART I

We are now in a position to use the evidence of this inscription in the study of the Athenian Calendar of the Fifth Century B. C. Already we have noticed that the generally accepted scheme of senatorial years as proposed by Keil cannot be correct. And we have shown that the senatorial years from 426-5 to 423-2 contained respectively 366, 368, 365, and 365 days. The natural assumption is that this same, or nearly the same, sequence obtained in the years immediately preceding 426 and in the years immediately following 422 B. C.

For the latter period a determination is possible with the help of the well known passage in Aristotle's *Constitution of Athens* where we learn that the new senate of the year 411 B. C. was due to enter office on the 14th day of Skirophorion ('Αθ. Πολ. XXXII, 1: ἔδει δὲ τὴν εἰληχυῖαν τῷ κυάμῳ βουλὴν εἰσιέναι τετράδι ἐπὶ δέκα Σκιροφοριῶνος). In other words, the first day of the first prytany of the senatorial year 411-0 was due to fall on the 14th day of Skirophorion in the civil year 412-1. In the year 422 we have from our inscription the further check between the two calendars that the 20th day of the tenth prytany coincided with the 23rd day of Skirophorion. We know further that in the year 423-2 the month of Skirophorion was full (*cf.* p. 77), and that the last prytany contained 36 days (*cf.* p. 16). Consequently the first day of the first prytany of the senatorial year 422-1 coincided with the 10th day of Hekatombaeon in the civil year 422-1.

We have now two dates where the correspondences between the civil and the senatorial years are known, and the eleven senatorial years from 422-1 to 412-1 inclusive contained the same number of days as fell between Hek. 10, 422-1 and Skir. 14, 412-1. We do not, *a priori*, know the sequence of ordinary and intercalary years in the civil calendar between these dates, but the following calculations may be made.

For the eleven civil years 422-1 — 412-1 inclusive, we may reckon five intercalary years and six ordinary years:

$$5 \times 384 + 6 \times 354 = 1920 + 2124 = 4044 \text{ days.}$$

or we may reckon four intercalary years and seven ordinary years:

$$4 \times 384 + 7 \times 354 = 1536 + 2478 = 4014 \text{ days.}$$

To obtain the corresponding number of days in the eleven years of the senatorial calendar we must subtract the first nine days of Hekatombaeon in 422-1 and the last 16 or 17 days of Skirophorion in 412-1, depending on whether Skirophorion was full or hollow. Even so there may be an element of error amounting to one or two days, because we have not counted on the possibility of intercalated days in the civil calendar between 422 and 411. For our purposes, however, it is sufficient to subtract $9 + 16 = 25$ from the total number of days in the eleven civil years (4044 or 4014) to obtain the total number of days in the eleven senatorial years. The possibilities are:

$$4044 - 25 = 4019$$
$$4014 - 25 = 3989$$

Since we have already observed that the years of the senatorial calendar from 426 to 422 average 366 days each, and since we expect a sequence of years approximating the solar calendar both before and after these dates, we may choose easily between the two figures above. With 4019 days in 11 years, each year contains an average of $365 \frac{4}{11}$ days; with 3989 days in 11 years, each year contains an average of $362 \frac{7}{11}$ days. Obviously the former is the correct solution and the civil calendar must be restored in accordance with it, with five intercalary years (or the equivalent) in the eleven years between 422-1 and 412-1 inclusive. It will be noticed that the average number of days in the senatorial calendar between these two dates is approximately the average of the solar year.

For the period preceding 422, the inscription *I.G.* I², 295 affords a point of departure in the year 433 B.C. We learn from this inscription that the first payment of money for the expedition to Corcyra was made on the 13th day of the first prytany by the treasurers of the sacred moneys of Athena for whom Krates was secretary, and that the second payment was made on the last day of the first prytany by the treasurers of the sacred moneys of Athena for whom Euthias was secretary. In other words, the board of treasurers, who held office from Panathenaea to Panathenaea, was changed between the 13th and the last day of the first prytany in 433 B. C.

We do not know whether this prytany contained 36 or 37 days, but we may choose the number of days most difficult for our problem, and say that the Panathenaic festival, *i.e.* Hek. 28 of the civil calendar, fell between the dates Pryt. I, 13 and Pryt. I, 36 in 433-2 B. C.

If now we reckon back from the fixed date Pryt. I, 1 = Hek. 10 in 422-1 we find that this period of 11 years must have contained four intercalary years in the civil calendar. We know, for example, that the four senatorial years 426-5—423-2 contained 1464 days. If we estimate the other 7 years as $7 \times 365 = 2555$ or as $7 \times 366 = 2562$ days we determine for the eleven year period the sum of 4019 or 4026 days. On the other hand the eleven years of the civil calendar contain $4 \times 384 + 7 \times 354 = 1536 + 2478 = 4014$ days, with the possibility that this figure is too small by one or two units because no account has been taken of possible intercalated days. To 4014 we must add the first 9 days of Hekatombaeon in 422-1 and we find that Hek. 1, 433-2 fell 4023 days before Pryt. I, 1, 422-1, while Pryt. I, 1, 433-2 fell from 4026 to 4019 days before the same terminus. In other words Pryt. I, 1, 433-2 fell between the third day from the end of Skirophorion 434-3 and the 5th day of Hekatombaeon 433-2.[1] And the Panathenaic festival on Hek. 28 fell between Pryt. I, 24 and Pryt. I, 31 of 433-2. Our reconstruction of the civil calendar between 433 and 422 with four intercalary years satisfies the epigraphical requirements of *I.G.* I², 295, which demands merely that Hek. 28 of 433-2 shall fall between Pryt. I, 13 and Pryt. I, 36-37. Conversely, Pryt. I, 1 of 433-2 must have fallen between Skir. 21 of 434-3 and Hek. 16 of 433-2.

These general determinations are fundamental for any study of the calendar, and with them in mind we may now turn our attention to the problem of discovering the character of the individual years.

It may be demonstrated, in the first instance, that 424-3 and 423-2 were ordinary years. In the argument of pp. 17-19 we sought to establish that the 26th day of the first prytany in 424-3 fell before the Panathenaic festival of that year, and we know from our reckoning of principal and interest from the payment made on that

---

[1] This limit appears as Hek. 9 in the table on p. 118, because two intercalated days have been inserted in the civil calendar during this interval of 11 years and the senatorial year 427-6 has been restored with less than the normal number of days.

date that the 26ᵗʰ day of the first prytany fell 705 days before the terminus to which interest was reckoned, *i.e.* 705 days before the last day of the last prytany in the senatorial year 423-2 (inclusive reckoning), and 705 days before the 9ᵗʰ of Hekatombaeon in the civil year 422-1, which gives the equivalent in the civil calendar.

Reckoning back from this terminus two ordinary civil years of 354 days each, we find that the 26ᵗʰ day of the first prytany in the senatorial year 424-3 fell on the 13ᵗʰ day of Hekatombaeon in the civil year 424-3 and consequently before the Panathenaic festival. On the other hand, if either of the civil years 424-3 or 423-2 were an intercalary year the 26ᵗʰ day of the first prytany in the senatorial year 424-3 would fall on the 13ᵗʰ day of Metageitnion in the civil year 424-3, and consequently after the Panathenaic festival of that year. This gives to us the proof that both 424-3 and 423-2 were ordinary years.

That 423-2 was an ordinary year may also be shown in the following way. There is given in the history of Thucydides (IV, 117-8) the text of a decree passed by the Athenian assembly fixing the terms of a truce with the Lacedaemonians in the spring of the year 423. From the preamble we learn that Akamantis was the prytanizing tribe at the time the decree was passed, and the first provision of the decree states that the truce was to last for one year from that very day, the 14ᵗʰ of Elaphebolion (τὴν δ'ἐχεχειρίαν εἶναι ἐνιαυτόν, ἄρχειν δὲ τήνδε τὴν ἡμέραν, τετράδα ἐπὶ δέκα τοῦ Ἐλαφηβολιῶνος μηνός). In our restoration giving the accounts of Athena for the year 424-3 we discovered that a payment of 100 Tal. was made on the 30ᵗʰ day of the eighth prytany. We were unable to restore the name of the prytanizing tribe, because either of the names Πανδιονίδος and Ἀκαμαντίδος fulfills the requirements of the spacing on the stone. But with the above passage of Thucydides in mind we may restore Ἀκαμαντίδος (line 33) and then demonstrate in the following way that the 14ᵗʰ of Elaphebolion falls in the eighth prytany.

We know that Pryt. I, 1 in 422-1 fell on Hek. 10. From this date we may reckon back 474 days to Pryt. VIII, 1 in 424-3 (*cf.* table p. 71 above). Counting 423-2 as an ordinary year we may also reckon back to the 14ᵗʰ of Elaphebolion as follows:

10 days	In Hekatombaeon of 422-1
354 days	Civil year 423-2
89 days	Last three months of 424-3
15 days	Days in Elaphebolion after the 14ᵗʰ.

468 days

The 14th of Elaphebolion fell six days after the first day of the eighth prytany and consequently we may formulate the following equation:

$$\text{Pryt. VIII, 7 (424-3)} = \text{Elaphebolion 14 (424-3)}$$

The restoration of the name Ἀκαμαντίδος in line 33 of *I.G.* I², 324 is justified, and we have a further proof that 423-2 was an ordinary year in the civil calendar. We may also make the interesting observation that within 24 days after the assembly had passed the armistice decree, a grant of 100 Tal. was made by the Athenian State for the conduct of the war. The truce was in fact a mere staying of the hand, but the troops remained in the field and their expenses had to be met.

The nature of the years of the civil calendar from 434-3 to 432-1 may be determined by studying the evidence of a Milesian parapegma, which fortunately has been in part preserved, in the light of our new knowledge about the character of the senatorial year.

The parapegma reads as follows: [1]

[θ]ερινῆς τρο[π]ῆς [γε]νομένης ἐπὶ Ἀψεύδους Σκιροφοριῶνος ‾ΙΓ‾,

ἥτις ἦν κατὰ τοὺς Αἰγυπτίους μία καὶ ‾Κ‾ τοῦ Φαμενώθ, ἕως [τῆ]ς

γενομένης ἐπὶ [Πολ]υκλείτου Σκι[ροφορι]ῶνος ‾ΙΔ‾,. κα[τὰ δὲ τοὺ]ς

Αἰγυπτί[ους τοῦ Παυ]νὶ τῆς ‾ΙΔ‾, [κατὰ δὲ τὸ Μιλ]ήσιον – – –

We find here that the summer solstice, which marked the beginning of the solar year, fell on the 13th day of Skirophorion in the year 433-2, *i.e.*, on exactly the same date which Diodorus gives (XII, 36) for the introduction of Meton's 19-year cycle. We have already seen that the senatorial year approximates very closely the solar year, and it is a striking confirmation of our calendar scheme that Pryt. I, 1 of the year 432-1 falls also on Skir. 13, 433-2 when we assume from 432 to 429 senatorial years of 366 days each and restore 433-2 as an intercalary year (*cf.* table p. 115 below).

Since it is clear from *I.G.* I², 295 that Pryt. I, 1 of 433-2 fell between Skir. 21 of 434-3 and Hek. 16 of 433-2 (*cf.* above p. 86) it is in fact only possible to have the summer solstice fall on Skir. 13 of 433-2 by assuming that the civil year 433-2 was intercalary. This argument I consider unassailable and the direct consequence of it is that the year 432-1 was itself ordinary, in spite of the arguments that have been

---

[1] *Cf.* Ferguson, The Athenian Calendar, *Clas. Phil.*, III (1908), p. 389 and also Diels and Rehm, *Sitzungsb. der Berliner Akademie*, 1904, pp. 92 ff.

advanced to the contrary.[1] We have also in *I.G.* I², 377 an indication that the year 434-3 was ordinary,[2] though this fact also is amply attested by the necessity of assuming that 433-2 was intercalary.

We may now return to the problem of the calendar character of the years 424-3 and 423-2 and show not only that these two years were ordinary but also that the year 425-4 was ordinary as well. The evidence lies in a reference made by a scholiast on the *Clouds* of Aristophanes (line 584) to an eclipse of the moon. The scholium reads as follows: ἔκλειψις ἐγένετο Σελήνης τῷ προτέρῳ ἔτει ἐπὶ Στρατοκλέους Βοηδρομιῶνι.

There is no need here to go into the question of the date of that part of the *Clouds* on which this comment was made, for the scholiast had in mind in any case the original production in 424-3, and his astronomical data pertain to the previous year 425-4 when Stratocles was archon. The eclipse of the moon to which he refers is that of October 9, 425 B.C.,[3] according to Julian reckoning, and consequently 104 days after the summer solstice of that year. Now the eclipse could have taken place only in the middle of the month, and we may reckon the date as on or near Boedromion 17, on account of the known divergence of two days between the lunar and the civil months.[4] By calculating back we find that the summer solstice fell on or near the 2nd day of Skirophorion, 426-5.

We discovered above that Pryt. I, 1 of the senatorial year, which corresponds approximately to the solar year, fell at the summer solstice of 432 when the senatorial years from 432-1 to 429-8 were restored as containing 366 days each. We know from our inscription that 426-5 was a year of 366 days. And so we know further that in the year 425-4 Pryt. I, 1 fell 3 days later than the summer solstice, that is, on Skir. 5 of 426-5.[5]

We may now reckon back from the known correspondence between the civil and the senatorial calendars in 422-1 (Pryt. I, 1 = Hek. 10) as follows (*cf.* table, p. 115):

425-4　Senatorial year　368 days　　Pryt. I, 1 = Skir.　5 (426-5)
　　　　Civil year　　　354 days

---

[1] *Cf.* Schmidt, *Handbuch der Griechischen Chronologie*, p. 188. But Schmidt's argument is based on a misinterpretation of Thucydides and is further vitiated because he has followed Boeckh's conclusions, now known to be false, based on a study of *I.G.* I², 324.

[2] Schmidt, *op. cit.*, p. 188. The fact that Ποσιδηιὼν μήν is mentioned (line 17) without the designation πρότερος or δεύτερος indicates that the year was ordinary.

[3] Schmidt, *op. cit.*, p. 186.

[4] Schmidt, *op. cit.*, p. 606.; also below, p. 105.

[5] I assume here that the ancient reckoning of the date of the solstice brings it to June 27, instead of June 28, as was also the case in 432. *Cf.* Unger, in Mueller's *Handbuch*, Vol. I. p. 738.

12

424-3	Senatorial year	365 days	Pryt. I, 1 = Skir. 19 (425-4)
	Civil year	355 days	
423-2	Senatorial year	365 days	Pryt. I, 1 — Skir. 29 (424-3)
	Civil year	354 days	
422-1			Pryt. I, 1 = Hek. 10 (422-1)

The required equation is obtained exactly if all three years 425-4, 424-3, and 423-2 were ordinary years in the civil calendar, while if any one of them were an intercalary year the eclipse would have fallen in Pyanepsion. We have here a proof not only that 425-4 was an ordinary year, but also the additional proof that 424-3 and 423-2 were ordinary years as well.

The dates given by the civil calendar in *I.G.* I², 63 are of interest at this point, because they belong to the year 425-4 when Stratocles was archon. We read here in lines 6-7:

hοῦτ[οι δὲ hορκοθέντες τõι] κοινõι h[όρκοι τ͂ες τάχσ]εος
πα[ρόντον μέχρι μενὸς Μαι]μακτεριõν[ος – – – – – – –]

and in lines 16-19:

hοι δὲ [ἐπιστατõντες τõμ πρυτά]νεον κα[θ]ιστάντον [ἐπάναγκες δικαστέριον
πλ͂ερες μ]ὲ ὄλεζον ͼ [χιλίος δικαστάς, ὅπος χσ]ὺν τ͂ει [βο]λ͂ει χσυντά[χσοσιν
τὸς φόρος τὸς ἐπὶ τ͂ες παλ]αιᾶς ἀρχ͂ες [μέχρι τ͂ες νομενίας τõ Π]ο[σ]ιδε[ιõ]νος
μενός· χ[ρεματιζόντον δὲ . . . . . .¹². . . . . . ἀ]πὸ νομενί[ας μέχρι νομενίας   ].

The restoration of the second passage conforms to our knowledge that the year was ordinary in the civil calendar, for mention is made of the month Posideion without the designation πρότερος or δεύτερος. The determination of the text of the document throughout is very difficult and there are many passages where the meaning is not entirely clear, though we are under the greatest obligation to Dr. Hiller von Gaertringen for his careful study which is embodied is the transcript as given in the *Corpus*. I suggest that the assessors of the tribute, to whom the first quotation above applies, were to report during the month of Maimakterion, and I should restore ἐντός in place of the word μέχρι of the *Corpus* in line 6. Partly on the basis of their reports the senate and a special judicial body were to determine the individual assessments, and I assume that their sittings were to continue through the month of Posideion, «from new moon to new moon» (lines 18-19). Perhaps in line 18 we should restore:

[μέχρι ἔνες καὶ νέας τõ Π]ο[σ]ιδε[ιõ]νος μενός

instead of:

[μέχρι τ͂ες νομενίας τõ Π]ο[σ]ιδε[ιõ]νος μενός.

Now we have already seen reason to believe (p. 26) that the decree was passed early in the fourth prytany of the year 425-4, because we know that the prytanizing tribe was Aegeis, which name we have restored in lines 18-19 of *I.G.* I², 324; and the expedition which was to set forth on the third day of the prytany (*I.G.* I², 63, line 34) was none other than the expedition of Demosthenes for which a payment of 30 Tal. was made on the third day of the fourth prytany (*I.G.* I², 324, lines 19-20).²

This was not, of course, the original expedition which set out from Athens in the spring of the year under Eurymedon and Sophocles, and which Demosthenes accompanied as a private citizen (*Cf.* Droysen, Bemerkungen über die Attischen Strategen, *Hermes,* 1875, pp. 17-19). The prytany date in question must be equated with October 21 in the Julian calendar (*cf.* tables on pp. 71 and 110) and the capture of Sphakteria, followed by the triumphal return of Cleon to Athens, was already an event of the past. Thucydides does not state whether Demosthenes returned with Cleon (IV, 39, 3), and yet the wording of our inscription implies that Demosthenes was in Athens when the payment was made in the fourth prytany. Ordinarily, when a payment was made for a general still in the field, the money was transferred through the hellenotamiae. When the payment was made directly to the generals, the presumption is that the generals were in Athens and that their expedition had not as yet set forth (*cf.* West, The Chronology of the Years 432 and 431 B.C., *Clas. Phil.,* 1915, p. 37). It is possible, of course, that the phraseology of our inscription is not exact, and that the money was paid over to the hellenotamiae for Demosthenes, who was still at Pylos. But it seems to me a far stronger probability that Demosthenes had returned to Athens with Cleon.¹ The time was ripe for his appearance, since he had proved that the public confidence shown in reëlecting him general had not been misplaced, and Eurymedon and Sophocles were strong enough to hold their position at Pylos (especially since the Athenians had taken more than a hundred hostages) until Demosthenes should return with a permanent garrison. I suggest, therefore, that the payment made in the fourth prytany was given directly to Demosthenes (*I.G.* I², 324, line 18) and that he sailed immediately for Pylos with a suitable force of occupation (*I.G.* I², 63, line 34; *cf.* also Thuc. IV, 41, 2). Soon after his arrival Eurymedon and Sophocles continued their interrupted journey toward Sicily (Thuc. IV, 46).²

---

¹ This suggestion finds some support in the phraseology of Thuc. IV, 37, 1: — ὁ Κλέων καὶ ὁ Δημοσθένης — — ἔπαυσαν τὴν μάχην καὶ τοὺς ἑαυτῶν ἀπεῖρξαν, βουλόμενοι ἀγαγεῖν αὐτοὺς Ἀθηναίοις ζῶντας — — .

² I do not agree with the suggestion of Hicks, *Greek Historical Inscriptions,* no. 16, that Demosthenes was still merely a private citizen. The suggestion is omitted from the second edition of the *Greek Historical Inscriptions* by Hicks and Hill.

While Demosthenes was preparing to consolidate the position won at Pylos, Cleon was developing his imperialistic schemes in Athens. One of his proposals was to secure ample funds by a heavier assessment of tribute from the Athenian allies, and it so happens that this measure came up for discussion in the assembly on the same day that Demosthenes and his fleet set out on their return for the Peloponnesus.

We have just determined above (p. 89) that in the year 425-4 Pryt. I, 1 fell on Skir. 5, 426-5, and we know that the first three prytanies of the year contained 37 days each (pp. 70-71). We may reckon then that Pryt. IV, 1 fell on or near Boedromion 27, and that the discussion after the προβούλευμα of the senate was opened in the assembly two days later, on Boedromion 29. Assessors were appointed who were to report during the month of Maimakterion and partly on the basis of their report the adjudication of the assessments was to proceed throughout the month of Posideion.

If 425-4, 424-3, and 423-2 are all restored as ordinary years in the civil calendar a period of approximately two months is allowed for the assessors to make their tour of the various tributary districts and report back to Athens, but if either of these years is construed as an intercalary year only one month, which is too short a time, may be allowed for the journey of the assessors.

The eclipse of the moon which occurred on Oct. 9, 425 B.C. and in the Attic month of Boedromion gives a point of comparison between the Attic civil year and the Julian calendar, and has been used by Oppert[1] to show that the year 426-5 was intercalary. The argument is sound and should not have been contested by Maltezos,[2] especially as it is confirmed by other astronomical data adduced by him for the year 427-6. Aristotle in the *Meteorologica* (p. 343, b. 4) refers to a comet which appeared at about the time of the winter solstice in the month of Gamelion of the year 427-6: ἐπὶ δ' ἄρχοντος Ἀθήνησιν Εὐκλέους τοῦ Μόλωνος ἐγένετο κομήτης ἀστὴρ πρὸς ἄρκτον, μηνὸς Γαμηλιῶνος, περὶ τροπὰς ὄντος ἡλίου χειμερινάς.

We have already observed that the summer solstice of the year 425 fell on or near the 2nd day of Skirophorion (p. 89) and we may reckon back one and one half years in the Julian calendar (or 548 days) to the winter solstice of the year 427-6. If we consider that 426-5 was an intercalary year, then 356 days had elapsed during that year before Skirophorion 2, and from Gamelion 1 to Skirophorion 29-30 in 427-6 may be reckoned as 177 days. In other words from the first day of Gamelion in 427-6 to the summer solstice of 425 was 356+177==533 days, and the first day

[1] J. Oppert, L'Année de Méton, *R.E.G.*, 1903, pp. 5-17, especially p. 11.
[2] Maltezos, Τὸ Ἀρχαῖον Ἀττικὸν Ἡμερολόγιον, Ἀρχ. Ἐφ., 1907, p. 244.

of Gamelion in 427-6 fell 15 days after the winter solstice of that same year. Under these conditions it is possible to understand how Aristotle may have referred to the appearance of the comet in the early days of Gamelion as near the time of the winter solstice. But if the year 426-5 is construed as an ordinary year the first day of Gamelion in the year 427-6 falls 45 days after the winter solstice and the statement of Aristotle is unintelligible. It may be noticed that we have here no evidence as to the calendar character of the year 427-6, because it is impossible to say at what date relative to the solar year the civil year began.

Certain determinations are also possible for the period following 422 B.C., for in *I.G.* I², 328 we have the evidence that in the year 414-3 both the 7th and the 25th of Gamelion fell in the seventh prytany. A second correspondence between the civil and the senatorial calendars is given by the equation derived from Aristotle's *Constitution of Athens* (XXXII, 1) that Pryt. I, 1 of 411-0 = Skir. 14 of 412-1. We also know that in the year 415-4 a payment of expense for the Panathenaic festival was made on the 20th day of the second prytany (*cf. I.G.* I², 302, lines 56-58).[1]

Keil was unable to make the correspondences in 415-4 and 414-3 fall into his scheme of the senatorial calendar, and he postulated here a time of confusion, while Schmidt (*Handbuch,* pp. 193-194) follows Boeckh in rejecting the evidence of the inscriptions as invalid. I propose, however, that we must adjust our calendar scheme to conform to the epigraphical evidence, especially since the requirements of the inscriptions are satisfied if 413-2 and 412-1 are construed as ordinary years.

From Pryt. VII, 1 in 414-3 to Pryt. I, 1 in 411-0 may be reckoned as 24 prytanies at the average rate of $36\frac{1}{2}$ days in each prytany to give the sum total of 876 days. At the same time from Gamelion 1 in 414-3 to Skir. 14 in 412-1 may be reckoned as $177 + 354 + 338$ days to give a total of 869 days. These figures may be claimed as correct within a day or two, which is sufficient for our purpose, and it is evident that Gamelion 1 falls on the 8th day of the seventh prytany in 414-3. Gamelion 7, therefore, falls on Pryt. VII, 14 and Gamelion 25 falls on Pryt. VII, 32.

This correspondence is also carried into the year 415-4 where we have evidence that a payment of expense for the Panathenaic festival was made on the 20th day of the second prytany. It may be demonstrated here that there was one intercalary year, and one only, between 415-4 and 412-1 inclusive.

From Pryt. I, 1 in 415-4 to Pryt. I, 1 in 411-0 may be reckoned as 1461 days ($365 + 366 + 365 + 365 = 4 \times 365\frac{1}{4} = 1461$). At the same time from Hek. 1 in 415-4 to Skir. 14 in 412-1 may be reckoned as 1430 days ($354 + 384 + 354 + 338 = 1430$).

---

[1] For the fact that these payments were made before the festival, *cf.* Keil, *Hermes,* XXIX (1894), pp. 40-41.

Pryt. I, 1 of 415-4 fell, consequently, 31 days before Hek. 1 of 415-4, *i.e.*, on Thargelion 29 of 416-5, which date is correct within a day or two, and Pryt. II, 1 fell on Hek. 6 or 7. The twentieth day of the second prytany, therefore, fell on Hek. 25 or 26 and so before the Panathenaic date Hek. 28. It is impossible to assume a second intercalary year in the civil calendar during this period without carrying Pryt. II, 20 of 415-4 into the month of Metageitnion, and if we assume that there was no intercalary year at all the payment recorded on the 20th day of the second prytany falls in Skirophorion, a month before the festival, and we have the further anomaly of four ordinary years of the civil calendar in succession.

Since we have just seen that 413-2 and 412-1 must be contrued as ordinary years so that Gamelion 7 and 25 may fall in the seventh prytany of 414-3, we know that either 415-4 or 414-3 must have been an intercalary year, and the validity of the equations just given is not affected whether we insert the intercalated month in the year 415-4 or 414-3. The computation proves that we must accept one of two possible sequences for the years 415-4 to 412-1:

	I	II
415-4	Intercalary	Ordinary
414-3	Ordinary	Intercalary
413-2	Ordinary	Ordinary
412-1	Ordinary	Ordinary

In either case the epigraphical requirements of *I.G.* I², 302 and 328 are satisfied.

In *I.G.* I², 304, lines 5-6, we have the account of a payment made for the Panathenaea in the year 410-9 which was credited in the second prytany of the year. This item may be used to build up further the sequence of years in the civil calendar and to prove, incidentally, that 411-0 was an intercalary year.

We may again take our departure from the equation derived from Aristotle's *Constitution of Athens* (XXXII, 1):

Pryt. I, 1 in 411-0 = Skir. 14 (412-1).

If 411-0 is an intercalary year, and if we assume 366 days in the senatorial year 411-0, we find that Pryt. I, 1 of 410-9 falls on Thargelion 26 in 411-0 (*cf.* table, p. 118). Pryt. II, 1 would fall 36 or 37 days later, on Hek. 3 or 4, and a payment made at any time between the 1st and 23rd days of the second prytany would consequently fall before the Panathenaic festival on Hek. 28. Our statement that 411-0 was an intercalary year is justified.

The attempt has been made recently by West to show that the payment for the Panathenaea was made after the festival, rather than before.[1] His argument is based on the fact that in *I.G.* I², 304 the treasurers of the year 410-9 made a payment for the Knights in the first prytany. If the payment in the second prytany was made before Hek. 28, then the payment in the first prytany must also have fallen before that date. This West claims to be impossible, because the treasurers of Athena are known to have held office from Panathenaea to Panathenaea. The argument would be valid if that part of *I.G.* I², 304 in question were merely a record of the treasurers of Athena, based on the year of the Panathenaic interval. But we are dealing here with a record of state expenses, not with a treasurers' record. We have already seen above (pp. 17-19) that these records of the state were based on the senatorial year, and consequently the possibility of payments recorded before the Panathenaic festival is not excluded. The same situation arises here that we found in dealing with the record of state expenses in *I.G.* I², 324 for the year 424-3. The year is dated by the eponymous archon, by the first secretary of the senate, and by the treasurers of the Goddess, of which methods of dating only the second is literally correct. A payment made between Pryt. I, 1 of 410-9 and Hek. 28 of 410-9 would indeed have been actually paid out by the treasurers of the year 411-0, as West claims, but the payment would have to be entered on the state books along with the expenses of the senatorial year 410-9 since the books of the previous year were closed on the last day of the preceding prytany. Hence an item actually paid by one board is listed in the state record as having been received from the succeeding board. Since the proofs given on pp. 86-92 for the calendar character of the civil years 425-4, 424-3, and 423-2, we are fortunate in having a specific instance in the first payment of war expenses for the year 424-3 (*I.G.* I², 324, line 28) where we know that the payment was made *before* the Panathenaic festival but where we find the record of the payment listed as though made by the treasurers who entered office at the time of the festival.

That the first part of *I.G.* I², 304 (lines 1-40) is a record of state expenses, and not merely a treasurers' record, is clear from the introductory formula Ἀθεναῖοι ἀνέλοσαν etc. in the first line of the inscription. It should be recognized, I believe, that the record of the treasurers proper, showing their transactions during the term of office from Panathenaea to Panathenaea — the record on which their audit was based — cannot properly have been introduced by the words «Expenditures of the Athenians», which can only mean the expenditures of the Athenian state. This applies

---

[1] West, Notes on Payments made by the Treasurers of Athena in 416-5 B. C., *A. J. A.*, XXIX (1925), pp. 10-11.

also to *I.G.* I², 293, 295, 296, 297, 298, and 302, all of which I interpret as state records, based upon the senatorial year. It may be noted also that the dates of individual payments are invariably given by the senatorial calendar.[1]

I.G. I², 305 is of a different character and may well contain the records of the treasurers for the year in which it is dated. The characteristic introductory formulae are not preserved, but it may be noted that the dates are given only by the civil calendar. It will be noted also that there is one date (line 7) at least as late as Hek. 21. If we are to assume that these accounts are based on the senatorial year (*i. e.* state accounts) we must assume that for some year during the latter part of the fifth century Pryt. I, 1 fell as late as Hek. 22. A glance at our table on pp. 118-120 will show that no such correspondence existed, and we must in consequence assume that the record in question was based on the year of the Panathenaic interval. It was in fact a treasurers' record in the sense in which West understands that term (*op. cit.*). But he includes *I.G.* I², 304 (lines 1-40) in the same category. It seems to me that we are dealing with two different kinds of document, and my argument that the second payment recorded in *I.G.* I², 304 fell before the Panathenaic festival of 410-9 follows this interpretation. I prefer to leave open the question of the character of the records preserved in *I.G.* I², 304, lines 41-92. The dates of payment are given both by the senatorial and the civil calendar and the accounts may have been reckoned on the basis of the Panathenaic year. But a judgment on this point is not essential to the argument outlined above.

We should notice in this connection a statement in Aristotle's *Constitution of Athens* (XXXIII) which indicates that 411-0 was a year of 12 months, *i. e.*, an ordinary year. Aristotle tells us that Mnasilochus was archon for two months in the year 412-1, and two months in the year 411-0, four months in all, while Theopompus was archon for the remaining ten months of 411-0. Keil has commented on this passage (*Hermes,* XXIX, 1894, p. 46, note) and shown, I believe correctly, that the reference to Theopompus as archon for «the other ten months» need not rest on any authoritative source, and that the figure may well have been obtained, without reference, merely by subtracting 2 from the conventional 12. It was the term of office of Mnasilochus in which Aristotle was interested rather than the term of office of Theopompus. The epigraphical evidence indicates that 411-0 was an intercalary year.

Keil (*Hermes,* XXIX, 1894, p. 39) adduced as proof that the year 410-9 was ordinary the fact that the last three prytanies contained 36 days each (*cf. I.G.* I², 304,

---

[1] I do not agree with West's restorations (*op. cit.*) for the year 416-5. *I.G.* I², 298 is an exception, for the dates are given by the civil month. But this inscription is from the archonship of Mnasilochus, when the senate of the ten prytanies had been suspended.

lines 29, 33, 39). We know from the inscription only that the last three prytanies contained *at least* 36 days each, and so I have from the beginning been inclined to question the correctness of this deduction. We now know, however, that there were no «ordinary» and «intercalary» years in the senatorial calendar, but that every senatorial year contained prytanies of 36 and 37 days, and we have here no direct proof of any kind as to the nature of the civil year 410-9. The character of the year may be determined, however, by the study of a very important series of cross-references between the civil and the senatorial calendars which appear in the inscription which was cut on the reverse side of the same stone. In *I. G.* I², 304, lines 42 ff., we have for the year 407-6 the following correspondences:

Pryt. II, 13 — —	Metageitnion 21	line 42
Pryt. II, 17 — —	Metageitnion 25	lines 44, 46
Pryt. II, 18 — —	Metageitnion 26	line 48
Pryt. II, 19 — —	Metageitnion 27	line 50
Pryt. II, 22 — —	Metageitnion 30	(last day) lines 51-52
Pryt. II, 23 — —	Boedromion 1	line 53
Pryt. II, 24 — —	Boedromion 2	line 55
Pryt. II, 26 — —	Boedromion 4	line 57
Pryt. II, 30 — —	Boedromion 8	lines 58-59, 60
Pryt. II, 36 — —	Boedromion 14	lines 62, 64.

These dates are sufficient to establish the fact that Hekatombaeon was hollow (29 days), Metageitnion full (30 days), Boedromion hollow (29 days), etc., and also to give the equation: Pryt. I, 1 = Hek. 1 for the year 407-6. The first day of the civil year here coincided with the first day of the senatorial year.

If we calculate down to this date, again taking our departure from the equation derived from Aristotle's *Constitution of Athens* (XXXII, 1):

Pryt. I, 1 in 411-0 = Skir. 14 in 412-1

we discover that there were no intercalary years between 410-9 and 408-7 inclusive. The parallel reckoning for civil and senatorial years is given as follows (*cf.* table p. 118 below):

Senatorial Year		Civil Year	
		16 days	Skir. 14—Skir. 29 (412-1)
366 days	411-0	384 days	411-0
366 days	410-9	354 days	410-9
366 days	409-8	355 days	409-8
365 days	408-7	354 days	408-7
1463 days		1463 days	

equated with the civil year is given in the Erechtheum building accounts, *I. G.* I², 374. In lines 108-112 we find that the architect received 37 Dr. as his salary for the sixth prytany and that the sub-secretary received 30 Dr. 5 obols.

μ-

ισθοί· Ἀρχιτέκτονι Ἀρχ[ιλόχ]-

οι Ἀργυλε͂θεν : ΔΔΔ⊓ΙΙ : ḥυ[πογρ]-

αμματεῖ Πυργίονι : ΔΔΔΙΙΙ[ΙΙ κεφ]-

άλαιον μισθο͂ : ⊠Δ⊓ΙΙ·ΙΙΙΙΙ.

It is evident that the rate per day was one drachma for the architect and five obols for the sub-secretary, and that the number of the days in the prytany was 37.

In lines 256-260 of the same inscription we find that the architect received 36 Dr. and the sub-secretary 30 Dr. for the eighth prytany:

μισθοί· Ἀρχιτέκτ-

ονι Ἀρχιλόχοι Ἀγρυλε͂θεν ΔΔ

Δ⊓Ι ḥυπογραμματεῖ Πυργίον-

ι ḥοτ[ρ]υνεῖ : ΔΔΔ κεφάλαιον μι-

σθο͂ ⊠Δ⊓Ι.

Here it is clear, with the same rate of pay, that there were 36 days in the eighth prytany. The significance of these figures in their relation to the number of days in the prytany was recognized by Kirchhoff and pointed out by him in the first edition of the *Corpus,* and it is pure sophistry on the part of Schmidt (*op. cit.,* p. 248) to attempt the proof that the evidence of this inscription indicates merely at least 37 and 36 days in the sixth and eighth prytanies. Work done by the day (καθ' ἡμέραν) is carefully distinguished in the text of the document itself from the salary (μισθός) given to the architect and the sub-secretary, and we must agree that their pay was reckoned on the basis of the exact number of days in the prytany.

So long as it was thought that the senatorial year was equated with the civil year and that the length of the prytany depended on whether the civil year was ordinary or intercalary it was of course difficult to reconcile these prytanies of 36 and 37 days with any calendar scheme, but they now take their place in the orderly succession of senatorial years, every one of which consists of prytanies of 36 and 37 days. It is perhaps superfluous to add that we have here no indication of any kind as to the nature of the civil year, though we have already demonstrated above (p. 97) that the year was ordinary.

PART II

Our study so far has been based upon evidence of an objective nature which admits little uncertainty or difference of opinion, but the problem to which we must now turn our attention, that of the calendar character of the year 422-1, has become involved, since Boeckh's time, in a network of subjective interpretation. In the course of the years it has been generally agreed that 422-1 was an ordinary year, either in its own right or because the intercalated month properly belonging to that year was omitted. Although Boeckh originally held that an extra month had been omitted from the theoretically intercalary year 421-0 he came eventually to the belief that the intercalary year was 422-1 and that the extra month had been dropped from the civil calendar in that year. This opinion is shared by Unger and Schmidt, who differ on so many other points in their reconstructions of the Athenian calendar in the Fifth Century.[1] Schmidt has adduced a considerable mass of evidence which proves, to his satisfaction, that the omission of a month took place in the year 422-1.

Our previous study of the calendar character of the individual years subsequent to 434-3 enables us, I believe, to make at this point a pertinent criticism against the method which has been universally employed by students of chronology in building up a calendar system for the latter part of the fifth century. It has been considered proved that Meton's 19-year cycle was not introduced into Athens in the year 432-1[2] because the supposedly known ordinary and intercalary years did not recur at intervals of 19 years.[3] But in place of Meton's cycle it has been universally assumed that the old 8-year cycle continued unchanged (as by Schmidt) or with some modification after 422-1 (as by Unger), although scholars have not been in agreement as to the exact sequence of ordinary and intercalary years which comprised the cycle. Every cycle has been constructed, however, under the assumption that the ordinary and intercalary years recurred at intervals of 8 years.

Now the same argument which has been used to prove that Meton's cycle was not introduced in 432-1 may be used to show that the 8-year cycle was not in use during the period in question, for the known ordinary and intercalary years did not recur at intervals of eight years. We discovered above (p. 88) that the year 433-2 was intercalary. If the 8-year cycle was continued past 432-1, not being affected by

---

[1] Unger, in *Mueller's Handbuch* I², pp. 750-751. Schmidt, *Handbuch der Griechischen Chronologie*, pp. 606-614.

[2] Except by Ferguson, The Athenian Calendar, *Clas. Phil.*, III (1908), pp. 386 ff.; and Fotheringham, Cleostratus, *J. H. S.*, 1919, pp. 176 ff.; also The Metonic and Callippic Cycles, *Monthly Notices of the Royal Astronomical Society*, 1924, pp. 383 ff.

[3] We may note in passing that our study above of the years from 434-3 to 407-6 has furnished an entirely new basis for comparison with the known dates of the fourth century.

the publication of Meton's calendar, then 425-4 should also be an intercalary year. But we have found (p. 90) that 425-4 was surely ordinary.

In a similar way, we have shown (p. 92) that 426-5 was an intercalary year. If the 8-year cycle was in force throughout this period of the Fifth Century, then 410-9 should also have been an intercalary year. But we have found (p. 97) that 410-9 was surely ordinary.

We have shown also that there were five intercalary years in the interval from 422-1 to 412-1 inclusive (p. 85), and since we have determined that there was only one intercalary year from 415-4 to 412-1 inclusive (p. 94) we know that there must have been four intercalary years between 422-1 and 416-5 inclusive. If the 8-year cycle, either the old cycle as maintained by Schmidt or the new cycle as maintained by Unger, was in effect during this period, then we should find the same sequence eight years later from 414-3 to 408-7. But we know that instead of four intercalary years during this latter interval there were at most only two (pp. 94 and 97).

We may note further that the three consecutive ordinary years from 425-4 to 423-2 (p. 90), the four intercalary years between 422-1 and 416-5, and the four consecutive ordinary years from 410-9 to 407-6 do not fall into place in any proposed scheme of the 8-year cycle.

The above cases may be cited as a *reductio ad absurdum* argument against the prevailing belief that a rigid 8-year cycle was in operation in Athens after 432-1, for the sequence of ordinary and intercalary years in any 8-year cycle fails utterly to conform to the known sequence of ordinary and intercalary years in the latter part of the Fifth Century. Our evidence seems to me conclusive that no cycle was employed with mathematical or astronomical exactness in the calendar which was actually used in Athens, but that considerable liberty was allowed the δῆμος in the disposition of the intercalary years within any given period.[1] We need now no longer hesitate to credit the statement of Diodorus about the publication of Meton's calendar scheme, merely because the ordinary and intercalary years after 432-1 do not recur at intervals of 19 years. It is highly probable that in actual practice the intercalation of extra months, before Meton's epochal date as well as after, depended on circumstances largely religious and political, over which the astronomer had no control. The great service of Meton's scheme was that it furnished a norm for the accurate measurement of time and an index by which the irregularity of the public calendar could be measured.

Perhaps we may assume that in general the effort was made to bring the lunar

---

[1] The arguments have been amply presented by Ferguson and Fotheringham, *op. cit.*, and need not be repeated here.

and solar periods into harmony at the end of each 19-year cycle. It is evident from the Milesian parapegma quoted above (p. 88) that this proper correspondence was effected in 110-9, at the end of the 17th Metonic cycle, but we may notice that there were eight intercalary years instead of seven in the first Metonic cycle, which extended from 432-1 to 414-3. We have determined above that there were four intercalary years between 433-2 and 423-2 (p. 86), and five intercalary years between 422-1 and 412-1 (p. 85). The two years 413-2 and 412-1 were ordinary years (p. 94) and the first intercalary year (433-2) fell just previous to the introduction of the Metonic cycle (p. 88).

Much has been written about the irregularity of the calendar during the latter part of the Archidamian war, and it has been generally assumed that the irregularity was caused by the «reform» of 422-1, when the extra month was omitted from one of the supposedly intercalary years. We may see, however, that the irregularity was of an entirely different character, caused not by the omission of a month, but rather by the insertion of a month. In this way we may explain the fact that four intercalary years occurred in the interval from 422-1 to 416-5, and the fact that Pryt. I, 1 fell on Hek. 10 in 422-1 while Pryt. I, 1 of 415-4 fell on or near Thargelion 29 of 416-5 (p. 94).

That there was discontent in Athens because of some anomaly in the calendar, especially among the conservative element, we may gather from the plays of Aristophanes, and two quotations must be here considered in this connection.

The first reference to the disturbed state of the calendar is found in the *Peace*, which was produced at the Greater Dionysiac festival of the year 421. Here we find the following conversation (lines 406-415) represented as taking place between Hermes and Trygaeus.

ΤΡΥΓΑΙΟΣ

ἡ γὰρ Σελήνη χὠ πανοῦργος Ἥλιος
ὑμῖν ἐπιβουλεύοντε πολὺν ἤδη χρόνον
τοῖς βαρβάροισι προδίδοτον τὴν Ἑλλάδα.

ΕΡΜΗΣ

ἵνα δὴ τί τοῦτο δρᾶτον;

ΤΡΥΓΑΙΟΣ

ὁτιή, νὴ Δία,
410   ἡμεῖς μὲν ὑμῖν θύομεν, τούτοισι δὲ
οἱ βάρβαροι θύουσι. διὰ τοῦτ' εἰκότως

βούλοιντ' ἂν ἡμᾶς πάντας ἐξολωλέναι,
ἵνα τὰς τελετὰς λάβοιεν αὐτοὶ τῶν θεῶν.

ΕΡΜΗΣ

ταῦτ' ἄρα πάλαι τῶν ἡμερῶν παρεκλεπτέτην;
415   καὶ τοῦ κύκλου παρέτρωγον ὑφ' ἁμαρτωλίας!

It is not necessary to assume with Van Leeuwen, Maltezos, and Schmidt[1] that these lines refer to the omission of a month in the year 422-1, for they may be amply explained by a variation between the civil months and the actual lunar cycle. Hermes implies that there was a grievance of some standing (another indication that the irregularity was not the omission of a month in 422-1) and we know from the evidence of the Milesian parapegma quoted above (p. 88) that in 432 the civil month varied from the true lunar month by two days (Schmidt, *Handbuch,* p. 606). The time of the solar eclipse of Aug. 3, 431 B.C. as given by Thucydides (II, 28: νουμηνίᾳ κατὰ σελήνην) also indicates that the civil month did not correspond exactly with the lunar cycle. If the variation had not been corrected by 422-1 it may well have given rise to the jest of Aristophanes about the connivance of the sun and the moon.

At all events the year 422-1 itself must have been an intercalary year, and certainly the passage from Aristophanes quoted above cannot be adduced to prove the contrary. If we assume for a moment that 422-1 was an ordinary year (*i. e.,* that the intercalated month was omitted) we find not only that we have from 425-4 to 422-1 a sequence of four ordinary years, but that from 421-0 to 416-5 four of the six years must have been intercalary; for we have just observed that the irregularity which came into the calendar between 422-1 and 416-5 was the insertion of an extra month, not the omission of one.

The next complaint of Aristophanes, which was voiced in the *Clouds,* is more specific, and indicates clearly, I think, the nature of the irregularity in the calendar. I quote from the antepirrhema of the parabasis, lines 615 ff.:

615   ἄλλα τ' εὖ δρᾶν φησιν. ὑμᾶς δ' οὐκ ἄγειν τὰς ἡμέρας
οὐδὲν ὀρθῶς, ἀλλ' ἄνω τε καὶ κάτω κυδοιδοπᾶν.
ὥστε ἀπειλεῖν φησιν αὐτῇ τοὺς θεοὺς ἑκάστοτε,
ἡνίκ' ἂν ψευσθῶσι δείπνου, καὶ ἀπίωσιν οἴκαδε
τῆς ἑορτῆς μὴ τυχόντες κατὰ λόγον τῶν ἡμερῶν.

[1] Van Leeuwen, commentary on the lines in question in his edition of the *Peace;* Maltezos, Τὸ Ἀρχαῖον Ἀττικὸν Ἡμερολόγιον, Ἀρχ. Ἐφ, 1907, p. 244; Schmidt, *Handbuch der Griechischen Chronologie,* p. 186.

620   κᾆθ᾽, ὅταν θύειν δέῃ, στρεβλοῦτε καὶ δικάζετε.
       πολλάκις δ᾽ ἡμῶν ἀγόντων τῶν θεῶν ἀπαστίαν,
       ἡνίκ᾽ ἂν πενθῶμεν ἢ τὸν Μέμνον᾽ ἢ Σαρπηδόνα,
       σπένδεθ᾽ ὑμεῖς καὶ γελᾶτ᾽, ἀνθ᾽ ὧν λαχὼν Ὑπέρβολος
       τῆτες ἱερομνημονεῖν καὶ ἔπειθ᾽ ὑφ᾽ ἡμῶν τῶν θεῶν
625   τὸν στέφανον ἀφῃρέθη. μᾶλλον γὰρ οὕτως εἴσεται
       κατὰ Σελήνην ὡς ἄγειν χρὴ τοῦ βίου τὰς ἡμέρας.

There is no question here of the omission or insertion of an extra month. The poet is merely noting the fact that the festival dates have become confused to such an extent that the gods do not know when their festivals are celebrated. The remedy proposed is that the Athenians should regulate their days by the moon. There could be, in my opinion, no more convincing evidence for the fact that the variation between the civil month and the lunar month still existed at the time of the production of the *Clouds*. The variation is astronomically attested in 433-2; reference is made to it by Thucydides in 431; and the complaints of Aristophanes a decade and more later refer to the same «long-standing» maladjustment of the calendar. My table of correspondences between the civil calendar and the Julian calendar (p. 120) shows the nature of this variation. Since the anomaly is known to have existed for ten or fifteen years subsequent to 432, I have made no adjustments with a view to bringing Hek. 1 to the actual date of the new moon. When this adjustment was made, and how, we do not know; but it must have been made at some time later than the date of the revised version of the *Clouds*.

There is nothing in either of the above passages quoted from Aristophanes to indicate either the insertion or the omission of an extra month. And yet we have found the proof elsewhere that an extra month was inserted in the civil calendar between 422-1 and 416-5 (p. 103).

The epigraphical evidence (*I.G.* I², 302 and 328) shows that the dislocation had not been corrected in 415-4 and 414-3, and from Aristotle's *Constitution of Athens* (XXXII, 1) we find that it still existed at the end of the year 412-1, where Skirophorion 14 equals Pryt. I, 1 (411-0).

If the inscription now given in the *editio minor* of the *Corpus* as *I.G.* I², 76 has been correctly dated in the year 423-2, we have also an epigraphical proof that 422-1 was an intercalary year, for in lines 53-54 of this inscription provision is made that the new archon shall intercalate the month of Hekatombaeon: μένα δὲ ἐμβάλλεν ℎεκατομβαιῶνα τὸν νέον ἄρχοντα. This provision appears in a «rider» moved by

14

Lampon and appended to the decree dealing with the consecration of first-fruits at Eleusis. The month of Hekatombaeon was to be intercalated apparently so that all the allies could be informed of the contents of the decree, with which they were bound to comply, and have time to bring their offerings to Eleusis before the Greater Mysteries in the fall. The date of the mysteries depended, of course, on the civil calendar and the intercalation of the month Hekatombaeon allowed 30 more days for the necessary compliance on the part of the allies with the provisions of the decree.[1]

We shall find later from our study of the evidence of Thucydides that it is impossible to assume *two* intercalated months in the year 422-1, so we must assume that if an extra month Hekatombaeon was added to the year the regulary intercalated month of Posideion must have been omitted. We still have left unexplained, however, the fact that an *extra* month was added between 422-1 and 416-5.

If the date assigned to the decree by Koerte is correct,[2] we may assume that it belongs to one of the years subsequent to the Peace of Nicias, perhaps, *e.g.*, 419-8, and that the extra month of Hekatombaeon was intercalated in the year 418-7. This would allow us to build up from 422-1 to 414-3 the following calendar scheme, including in this period the necessary five intercalary years.

422-1	I	
421-0	O	
420-9	O	
419-8	I	
418-7	I	(properly an ordinary year)
417-6	I	
416-5	O	
415-4	O	
414-3	I	

I have given this hypothetical sequence in the table on p. 118, irrespective of the date of *I.G.* I², 76, which is too uncertain to be of real value in our discussion. Tanner, for example (*Clas. Phil.*, XI, pp. 65 ff.), has dated the decree in the year 443.

Whatever the way in which the irregularity may have arisen we may be sure that an extra month was inserted into the calendar at some time between 422-1 and

---

[1] That the decree was passed late in the year is evident from the necessity of intercalating the extra month Hekatombaeon, and also from the haste with which the messengers were to be sent out to the allies (line 23) and from the reference to the ninth prytany (line 60).

[2] Koerte, *Ath. Mitt.*, XXI, 1896, pp. 320-332. Koerte has recently restated his argument in favor of one of the years after the Peace of Nicias. *Cf.* Noack's Eleusis, pp. 313-317.

416-5, so that the first Metonic cycle contained eight intercalary years instead of seven. This dislocation of the civil year in its proper relation to the solar year was corrected, however, at the beginning of the second Metonic cycle, for we have found that 411-0 was an intercalary year followed by four ordinary years (pp. 94 and 98) This irregularity is the counterpart of that introduced earlier into the calendar and in part they explain each other.

I have endeavored to point out above that the evidence of Aristophanes does not indicate the omission of a month from the civil calendar in the year 422-1. But other arguments have also been brought into play to prove that a month was omitted, and these must be here considered. The 8-year cycle, for example, as constructed by Schmidt, demanded 20 intercalary years between 432-1 and 382-1 inclusive, and his assumption that one of the intercalated months had been omitted (cf. op. cit., p. 611) was necessary in order to satisfy the evidence of Ptolemy (Almagest, 4, 10, p. 275 ff.), who gives the date of two eclipses in 383-2 as during the months of Posideion and Skirophorion, and of one eclipse in 382-1 as in the month of Posideion I. If one of the intercalated months were not omitted, the eclipses would have fallen in Maimakterion and Thargelion of 383-2 and in Maimakterion of 382-1.

But if we allow that Meton's 19-year cycle was instituted in the year 432-1, we find that there were 8 intercalary years in the first cycle and 6 intercalary years in the second, where both the irregularity and the correction are epigraphically attested, and that in the third cycle there were five intercalary years between 394-3 and 382-1. In other words there were only 19 intercalary years between 432-1 and 382-1, and the dates of the eclipses in 383-2 and 382-1 are correct as given by Ptolemy without the assumption that a month was omitted. Schmidt's scheme created an anomaly which had to be explained, and lent a certain plausibility to his interpretation of Thucydides and Aristophanes, wherein their texts are used as evidence not only for the proposition that a month had been omitted, but also for the time when the omission was made.

Since our calendar scheme indicates that no month was omitted between 432-1 and 382-1 we may see that the weight of the arguments from Thucydides and Aristophanes is considerably impaired. I believe also that the chronological data given by Thucydides have been generally misinterpreted, largely because of the mistaken belief that a month had been omitted at some time between 432-1 and 405-4. The study of Thucydides has been complicated by the fact that the text has in places suffered evident corruption in transmission, but the proper emendations are clear and have already been satisfactorily made.

The date for the beginning of the war, for example, is given as follows (Thuc. II, 1): ———— καὶ Πυθοδώρου ἔτι δύο μῆνας ἄρχοντος Ἀθηναίοις μετὰ τὴν ἐν Ποτιδαίᾳ μάχην μηνὶ ἕκτῳ καὶ ἅμα ἦρι ἀρχομένῳ Θηβαίων ἄνδρες ——— ἐσῆλθον ———— ἐς Πλάταιαν.

The numeral δύο has been with general consent corrected to τέσσαρας with the assumption that the reading is a corruption of δ´, and the attack on Plataea must be dated in the latter part of the month Anthesterion rather than in the latter part of the month Munichion.[1]

Secondly, the date of the Peace of Nicias is given as ten years and some days after the first incursion into Attica and the outbreak of the war (Thuc. V, 20): Αὗται αἱ σπονδαὶ ἐγένοντο τελευτῶντος τοῦ χειμῶνος ἅμα ἦρι ἐκ Διονυσίων εὐθὺς τῶν ἀστικῶν αὐτόδεκα ἐτῶν διελθόντων καὶ ἡμερῶν ὀλίγων παρενεγκουσῶν ἢ ὡς τὸ πρῶτον ἡ ἐσβολὴ ἡ ἐς τὴν Ἀττικὴν καὶ ἡ ἀρχὴ τοῦ πολέμου τοῦδε ἐγένετο.

Here again it is evident that the ten years and some days must be reckoned from the actual outbreak of the war, i. e., the attack on Plataea, rather than from the first incursion into Attica,[2] which took place about 80 days later (Thuc. II, 19, 1).

Otherwise the text of Thucydides is sound, though chronological difficulties have been created by the attempt to make it conform to a rigid calendar scheme and the attempt to interpret with too much exactitude the general statements of the author. When Thucydides says (V, 26) that the entire war lasted for 27 years and some additional days he is thinking of the commencement of hostilities late in Anthesterion of 432-1 and of the final debacle in Munichion of 405-4. Whether Thucydides reckoned by the actual solar year, or the senatorial year, or by the civil year, or merely by summers and winters, as he himself says he reckoned (V, 20), this period of time amounts to 27 years and some additional days. It seems to me that Schmidt (*Handbuch,* pp. 190-193 and 611-613) is forcing the evidence when he tries to prove that Thucydides reckoned with a solar year, and when he insists that the 19 extra days determined by his calculation over and above the 27 years may properly be called ἡμέρας οὐ πολλάς, while 49 days may not be properly so called. Whether or not 49 days are οὐ πολλαί is entirely a matter of subjective interpretation, and we have

---

[1] *Cf.* Schmidt, *Handbuch,* pp. 388-389. It is not necessary here to discuss the reading μηνὶ ἕκτῳ (*cf.* West, The Chronology of the Years 432 and 431 B. C., *Clas. Phil.,* 1915, pp. 34-53, especially pp. 46 ff.) or to consider West's suggestion that the numeral δύο be amended to read πέντε. This latter suggestion by West was made necessary in the development of his thesis by the assumption that Keil's calendar scheme for the fifth century was correct. The study, here mentioned, of the chronology of the early days of the Peloponnesian war must be revised in the light of our new knowledge concerning the Athenian calendar.

[2] *Cf.* Schmidt, *op. cit.,* p. 190; note on Thuc. V, 20 in Classen's edition.

no evidence from Thucydides' report of the length of the war, as Schmidt proposes, to justify the assumption that a month had been omitted between 432 and 404. Such a conclusion depends not only on the subjective interpretation pointed out here, but it implies also an exact method of reckoning quite different from the computation of summers and winters which Thucydides established as his norm. These Thucydidean seasons were elastic. Θέρος comprised also spring (IV, 117) and fall (II, 31), although spring and fall were transition periods and sometimes associated with the winter half of the year (V, 20). It may indeed be assumed that these periods were determined by the phenomena of the solar year, warmth and cold, growth and harvest of crops, etc., though it would again be a forced interpretation to attempt the equation of any of the seasons with definite dates in the solar or the civil years.

In a similar way Schmidt's argument that an intercalated month had been omitted between 432 and 421 seems to me unconvincing (*op. cit.*, pp. 190-193) in spite of the assurance with which it is urged.

On the other hand, the argument that the Peace of Nicias cannot have been ratified at the beginning of May is of a different nature altogether (Schmidt, *op. cit.*, p. 190) although to avoid this anomaly of date, it is not necessary to assume, as Schmidt does, that the intercalated month properly belonging to the year 422-1 was omitted. The date is given by Thucydides as «at the close of winter and the beginning of spring immediately after the Dionysiac festival», and it is quite true that we cannot reckon the end of the winter season as early in May.

If reference is made to our table of correspondences between the civil year and the Julian calendar (p. 118) it will be found that July 3 = Pryt. I, 1 = Skir. 21 in the year 421 B. C. This equation is based on our foregoing study of the calendar, without the assumption that the intercalated month was omitted from 422-1. Now the 25th day of Elaphebolion, which is given by Thucydides as the date of the Peace (V, 19) fell 85 days before this date or on the 9th of April. This date agrees perfectly with the evidence of Thucydides as to the time of the year. In Schmidt's scheme one mistake was corrected by another, for it was necessary to assume the omission of a month to bring the incorrect correspondences between the civil and the solar years into harmony with Thucydides.

Certain events in the year 432-1 may now also be discussed in the light of the table given below (p. 118). We know that the attack on Plataea occurred toward the end of the month Anthesterion in the dark of the moon,[1] perhaps, let us say,

---

[1] There is no assurance that Boeckh's assumption (*Zur Gesch. d. Mondcyclen*, p. 78) is correct, that the four months (Thuc. II, 2, 1) should be reckoned exactly and that the attack occurred on the last day of Anthesterion.

on the 25ᵗʰ.[1] About 80 days later (inclusive reckoning) came the invasion of Attica, on or near the 16ᵗʰ day of Thargelion, which corresponds to May 20 in the Julian calendar (table p. 118). Thucydides says that the incursion was made τοῦ θέρους καὶ τοῦ σίτου ἀκμάζοντος which I interpret as meaning during the summer and while the grain was full. Perhaps the grain was ready for the harvest — the words do not necessarily imply that the harvest was in progress — and this condition of the grain corresponds to the date of May 20ᵗʰ.[2]

Thucydides also says that while the Spartan forces were in Attica (II, 23, 2: ὄντων δὲ αὐτῶν ἐν τῇ γῇ οἱ Ἀθηναῖοι ἀπέστειλαν τὰς ἑκατὸν ναῦς) the fleet of 100 ships under Karkinos and Proteas and Socrates was sent out to ravage the Peloponnesus. In *I.G.* I², 296, lines 30 ff., we have the record of expenses paid for this expedition, beginning with a direct payment to the generals before their departure on the 8ᵗʰ day before the end of the ninth prytany (inclusive reckoning). By reference again to the table on p. 118 we find that in 431-0 Pryt. I, 1 = Hek. 1. Now since the 8ᵗʰ day before the end of the ninth prytany in 432-1 fell 44 days before Pryt. I, 1 of 431-0 it must be equated with Thargelion 16ᵗʰ in the civil calendar, which, as we have seen above, corresponds to May 20ᵗʰ in the Julian calendar.

The computation is of interest because it shows that the first payment for the fleet which set out to ravage the Peloponnessus was made during the first few days of the Spartan invasion of Attica. The account given by Thucydides (II, 21-23) implies that the departure of the fleet took place some time after the incursion of the Spartans, in fact, only shortly before their withdrawal through Boeotia. If this interpretation is correct then we must assume that the payments made for the expenses of the fleet and given to the hellenotamiae during the latter part of the ninth and early part of the tenth prytanies were made while the fleet was still in Piraeus. The time relation of events indicated by Thucydides suggests that the fleet did not set forth until perhaps the middle of the tenth prytany. The argument has been advanced, however, that the fleet actually departed immediately after the first payment to the generals, and the fact that the hellenotamiae, not the generals in command, received the amounts of the second and third payments has been urged as proof that the generals were no longer in Athens.[3]

I am not sure that this proof is sound. One may well concede that when the money was paid directly to the generals, the generals were themselves in Athens. The

---

[1] The date cannot be fixed exactly. The attack may have taken place on any one of the latter days of the month.

[2] *Cf.* West, The Chronology of the Years 432 and 431 B. C., *Clas. Phil.*, 1915, p. 40.

[3] West, *op. cit.*, pp. 37, 38-41.

corollary does not necessarily follow, that when the money was paid to the hellenotamiae the generals were not in Athens. A case in point is the record of the second payment to the hellenotamiae for the expenses of the army in Macedonia during this same year (*I.G.* I², 296, lines 11-13). Phormio must have been in Athens at the time the payment was made, for he took the money with him to Macedonia. And Phormio, as the general who went to take the place of the fallen Nicias, must have been the one to render an account of how the money was spent. Yet the money was transferred from the treasury to the hellenotamiae and then to Phormio, even while he was still in Athens. I prefer to believe that the payments recorded in *I.G.* I², 296 as having been made through the hellenotamiae for the expenses of the fleet which ravaged the Peloponnesus were made before the fleet departed, rather than to assume that the fleet set sail immediately after the first payment to the generals, with the necessary consequence that the time relation between the invasion of Attica and the departure of the fleet, as given by Thucydides, must be revised.

From Thucydides also we have a further control over the observations which have been made above on the character of the civil year 422-1, for two events from the years 423 and 421 are dated both according to the Athenian and the Spartan calendars. The Truce of Brasidas was sanctioned by the Athenian assembly on Elaph. 14, 423 and sworn to by the Spartans on Gerastios 12, 423 (Thuc. IV, 118-9). There has been general agreement among students of chronology that these dates are identical,[1] although that fact is not made explicitly clear by the narrative of Thucydides. The date of the ratification of the Peace of Nicias (Thuc. V, 19) is also given as Elaph. 25, 421 by the Athenian calendar and as Artemisios 27, 421 by the Spartan calendar. The correspondences here indicated between the calendar systems of Athens and of Sparta have been often discussed[2] and since the time of Boeckh it has been agreed that in Athens the two ordinary years 423-2 and 422-1 corresponded to the two years 423-2 and 422-1 at Sparta, one of which was ordinary and one intercalary.[3] In this way it has been explained how Elaphebolion should correspond to the month Gerastios in 423 and to the month Artemisios in 421, Artemisios preceding Gerastios in the Spartan calendar. But the evidence needs to be reëxamined, for while we have proved above in three different ways (pp. 86-92) that the year 423-2 was ordinary in the Attic calendar, we have also shown that the intercalated month cannot have been omitted from the year 422-1.

---

[1] Schmidt, *Handbuch*, p. 222. My own conviction is that these dates do not correspond exactly.

[2] *Cf.* Schmidt, *l. c.*, and references there cited.

[3] Boeckh, Zur Geschichte der Mondcyclen der Hellenen, *Besonderer Abdruck aus den Jahrbüchern für classische Philologie*, Suppl. N. F. Bd. I, Heft 1, pp. 86-92 (Leipzig 1855).

But if either 423-2 or 422-1 is an intercalary year in the Attic calendar, the accepted explanations of the correspondence with the Spartan calendar must be abandoned, because in that case two intercalary years would there follow in succession.

The fundamental difficulty is that everyone has followed Boeckh in transposing the months Gerastios and Artemisios in the Spartan calendar.[1] This was necessary so long as he considered it certain that the Attic years 423-2 and 422-1 were both ordinary, and the proof of this fact, as Boeckh considered it, lay partly in his deductions from the inscription which we have been considering in this book. But we now know that Boeckh's restorations of this inscription are not correct, and we must also free ourselves from the consequences of his restorations as they involve the Spartan calendar. In particular, we may still agree with Hermann that the Spartan month Gerastios preceded Artemisios, and the correspondences between the Attic and the Spartan calendars may be given accordingly.[2]

If we allow that the two years 423-2 and 422-1 were ordinary years in the Spartan calendar, then from Gerastios of 424-3 to Artemisios of 422-1 was an interval of 25 months. In Athens we know that the year 423-2 was ordinary, but the required interval between Elaphebolion 424-3 and Elaphebolion 422-1 may only be obtained if we consider that the year 422-1 was intercalary, as we have argued above.

Remembering that Pryt. I, 1 = Hek. 10 in 422-1 we may estimate the date of the civil year on which Pryt. I, 1 of 421-0 will fall. If the senatorial year 422-1 contained 366 days, Pryt. I, 1 of 421-0 fell (384-10)-366 = 8 days before the end of the civil year 422-1. That is, Pryt. I, 1 of 421-0 = Skir. 21 of 422-1 (cf. tables, pp. 118-120).

This conclusion seems to be at variance with an inference which has been drawn from Attic inscriptions of the year 421-0 in which support has been claimed for Keil's discovery that the civil years and the senatorial years were not coterminous throughout the Fifth Century. Keil's discovery remains of fundamental importance and is one of his lasting contributions to the study of the Athenian Calendar, but I cannot concede that the inscriptions cited from the year 421-0 bear on the question either for or against his proposition.[3]

---

[1] Boeckh, op. cit.

[2] K. F. Hermann, Über Griechische Monatskunde, p. 124, first proposed that Gerastios fell before Artemisios. Boeckh changed the order to comply with his calendar scheme.

[3] Cf. West, Notes on Payments made by the Treasurers of Athena in 416-5 B. C., A. J. A., XXIX (1925), pp. 3-16, especially p. 13, note 2. West's objections to Keil's calendar scheme are valid, but they do not disprove his main thesis: that the senatorial year was not coterminous with the civil year.

The problem, briefly stated, is as follows. From *I.G.* I², 311 we learn that Prepis was first secretary of the senate in the year of the archon Aristion, 421-0. We learn also from *I.G.* I², 370 that Menekles was first secretary of the senate in the year of Aristion, 421-0, and this fact is confirmed by the preamble of *I.G.* I², 220, where the name of Menekles is to be restored (*cf.* West καὶ Meritt, Ὁ Φορολογικὸς Κατάλογος τοῦ 421-0, ᾿Αρχ. ᾿Εφ., 1924, p. 48). It has been argued that the year of the senate for which Prepis was first secretary is different from the year of the senate for which Menekles was first secretary, and that the year of Prepis was 422-1, the year of Menekles being 421-0.[1] Since both names appear under the archonship of Aristion, which began on Hek. 1, 421-0, the assumption is that the senatorial year 422-1 continued at least into Hekatombaeon of 421-0.

In the first place it is not a certain premise that the years of Prepis and Menekles are distinct. Prepis may well have been secretary in the first prytany of 421-0, in which office he was succeeded by Menekles because of illness or death or some disqualification of which we have no record, and we may expect to find published documents from the year 421-0 bearing either the name of Prepis or of Menekles as first secretary. But the insuperable objection to the accepted interpretation seems to me to be the fact that if Prepis was first secretary for the senatorial year 422-1, then we have no record of receipts from the first fruits at Eleusis for 421-0. The record of the year 420-19 would follow immediately upon that of the year 422-1. In the highly problematical case that there were no receipts in 421-0 we should expect some mention of that fact. *Cf. I.G.* I², 370, where the statement that no moneys were received is made for those years in which there were no receipts. To this may be added the less serious but still real objection that it would be unduly naive to refer to the receipts of the year for which Prepis was secretary (422-1) as under the archonship of Aristion (421-0), when, according to the theory, Aristion could have been archon for only a short part, perhaps less than a month, of the year which went under the name of Prepis.

I propose that the correct interpretation of these inscriptions is that Prepis and Menekles were both «first secretaries» of the year 421-0 and that for some reason unknown to us Menekles succeeded Prepis before the end of the first prytany. We have here no evidence of any kind as to the correspondences between the civil and the senatorial calendars in the first month of 421-0, and the equation

$$\text{Pryt. I, 1 of 421-0} = \text{Skir. 21 of 422-1}$$

[1] *S. E. G.*, Vol. II, no. 3, and note; *Cf.* also note on *I.G.* I², 324 in the *editio minor* of the *Corpus*, Vol. I, p. 156.

need not be challenged because of the evidence of *I.G.* I², 220, 311, and 370.[1]

I am indebted to Professor Allen B. West for suggesting to me still another argument in favor of considering 422-1 as an intercalary year. Cleon set out from Athens on his campaign against Brasidas in the late summer or early autumn of 422, after the Pythian festival (Thuc. V, 1-2). This fell in the Delphic month of Boukatios, which corresponds to Metageitnion in the Athenian calendar. We know also from Eratosthenes, quoted by a scholiast on the *Peace* of Aristophanes (line 48) that Cleon perished before Amphipolis eight months before the production of the play at the Greater Dionysia in Elaphebolion. Reckoning inclusively, the date of Cleon's death may be set as Metageitnion if the year 422-1 was ordinary, or as Boedromion if the year was intercalary. But the time which must have been consumed by Cleon in his journey from Athens to Macedonia, touching at Skione and Torone, and recovering for Athens numerous small towns on the coast of the Macedonian peninsula and beyond the Strymon before the battle at Amphipolis, necessitates the later date.[2] Sufficient time for Cleon's expedition is also allowed if we assume that *I.G.* I², 76 should be dated in 423-2 and that an extra Hekatombaeon was intercalated in 422 (*cf.* p. 105). In this case the Pythian festival would fall in the second Hekatombaeon, and Cleon's death could be dated in Metageitnion. But in any case the indications are that 422-1 was a year of 13 months in the civil calendar.

PART III

The following table is presented to show my first draft of the relations between the senatorial and the civil years during the latter part of the Fifth Century and their correspondences with the Julian calendar. The sequence of ordinary and intercalary years in the civil calendar is given as determined in our study so far. Where the character of the year has been restored for the purpose of making the table, this fact is indicated by parentheses.

---

[1] Menekles was from the deme of Anaphlystos (*I.G.* I², 370) which belonged to the tribe Antiochis. We know of Prepis merely that he did not belong to the tribe Aegeis, because he was secretary while this tribe held the prytany (*I.G.* I², 81). *Cf.* Ferguson, The Athenian Secretaries, *Cornell Studies in Classical Philology*, No. VII, 1898, p. 26. It may be significant, however, that both of these names are found in a catalogue which must be dated about 450 B. C. (*I.G.* I², 933). Unfortunately we do not know the nature of the catalogue, but it is probable that the Athenians there listed (not all of the names are Athenian) belonged to one tribe, and the names Menekles and Prepis are sufficiently uncommon to lend some support to the argument presented above, namely, that the Menekles and Prepis with whom we have to deal in 421 belonged also to the same tribe.

[2] For Cleon's conquests in this expedition *cf.* West and Meritt, Cleon's Amphipolitan Campaign and the Assessment List of 421, *A.J.A.*, XXIX (1925), pp. 59-69.

Date of Attic Year	Julian Intercalation	Senatorial Year	Civil Year	Attic Intercalation	Correspondences between the Julian, senatorial, and civil calendars
434-3	I	366	354	O	June 27 — Pryt. I, 1 — Skir. 21 (435-4)
433-2	O	365	384	I	June 27 — Pryt. I, 1 — Hek. 3
432-1	O	366	354	O	June 27 — Pryt. I, 1 — Skir. 13 (433-2)
431-0	O	366	354	(O)	June 28 — Pryt. I, 1 — Skir. 25 (432-1)
430-29	I	366	384	(I)	June 29 — Pryt. I, 1 — Hek. 8
429-8	O	366	355	(O)	June 29 — Pryt. I, 1 — Skir. 20 (430-29)
428-7	O	365	384	(I)	June 30 — Pryt. I, 1 — Hek. 1
427-6	O	365	354	(O)	June 30 — Pryt. I, 1 — Skir. 11 (428-7)
426-5	I	366	384	I	June 30 — Pryt. I, 1 — Skir. 22 (427-6)
425-4	O	368	354	O	June 30 — Pryt. I, 1 — Skir. 5 (426-5)
424-3	O	365	355	O	July 3 — Pryt. I, 1 — Skir. 19 (425-4)
423-2	O	365	354	O	July 3 — Pryt. I, 1 — Skir. 29 (424-3)
422-1	I	366	384	I	July 3 — Pryt. I, 1 — Hek. 10
421-0	O	366	354	(O)	July 3 — Pryt. I, 1 — Skir. 21 (422-1)
420-19	O	366	354	(O)	July 4 — Pryt. I, 1 — Hek. 4
419-8	O	365	384	(I)	July 5 — Pryt. I, 1 — Hek. 16
418-7	I	366	384	(I)	July 5 — Pryt. I, 1 — Skir. 27 (419-8)
417-6	O	365	384	(I)	July 5 — Pryt. I, 1 — Skir. 8 (418-7)
416-5	O	365	355	(O)	July 5 — Pryt. I, 1 — Tha. 19 (417-6)
415-4	O	365	354	O	July 5 — Pryt. I, 1 — Tha. 29 (416-5)
414-3	I	366	384	I	July 5 — Pryt. I, 1 — Skir. 11 (415-4)
413-2	O	365	354	O	July 5 — Pryt. I, 1 — Tha. 22 (414-3)
412-1	O	365	354	O	July 5 — Pryt. I, 1 — Skir. 3 (413-2)
411-0	O	366	384	I	July 5 — Pryt. I, 1 — Skir. 14 (412-1)
410-9	I	366	354	O	July 6 — Pryt. I, 1 — Tha. 26 (411-0)
409-8	O	366	355	O	July 6 — Pryt. I, 1 — Skir. 9 (410-9)
408-7	O	365	354	O	July 7 — Pryt. I, 1 — Skir. 20 (409-8)
407-6	O	365	354	O	July 7 — Pryt. I, 1 — Hek. 1
406-5	I	365	384	(I)	July 7 — Pryt. I, 1 — Hek. 12
405-4	O	365	354	(O)	July 6 — Pryt. I, 1 — Skir. 22 (406-5)

This table is presented with the full realization that it contains many uncertainties of detail. We know, for example, that June 27 of the Julian calendar fell on Skir. 13 in 432 B.C., because this was the supposed date of the summer solstice (*cf.* p. 104 and p. 119 below), but we do not know that this date also corresponded to Pryt. I, 1. The relatively regular correspondence between the senatorial calendar and the solar year after 422-1 indicates that perhaps the senatorial year began later than the summer solstice in 432, in other words, that the number of days in the senatorial years from 433-2 to 427-6 has been reckoned too high. The senatorial year 425-4 contained three more than the normal number of days (*cf.* table p. 70) and to keep the average of $365\frac{1}{4}$ days per year we should perhaps restore one of the earlier years with less than the normal.

If 427-6 is restored as a year of 362 days—and this can be done without destroying the sequence of 36 and 37 day prytanies within the year—this variation can be corrected. The earlier years from 433 to 427 may also be restored with an average of $365\frac{1}{4}$ days without violating the evidence offered by *I.G.* I², 295 that Hek. 28 of 433-2 must fall between Pryt. I, 13 and Pryt. I, 36-37, and without destroying the validity of our argument that 433-2 must have been an intercalary year (*cf.* p. 88).

There is too much uncertainty about the time of intercalation of extra days and the sequence of full and hollow months in the civil year to allow the assumption that the correspondences between the senatorial and civil calendars in the following tables are correct to the day. But it will be noticed that the tables have been drawn up in such a way that the order of full and hollow months within the year changes with each intercalary year, and that it agrees with what evidence we have for the order of months in individual years:

1. In 423-2 Hekatombaeon was hollow and Skirophorion full (*cf.* p. 77).
2. In 419-8 Hekatombaeon was full (*cf.* p. 121).
3. In 407-6 Hekatombaeon was hollow, etc. (*cf.* p. 97).

The main features, however, are clear and well established, especially the fact that the senatorial year approximated the solar year. To my mind this consideration outweighs the probability that Pryt. I, 1 should be equated with Skir. 13 in 432, especially since we observe that in any case the senatorial year did not begin until about a week after the summer solstice in most of the years of the preceding table. The revised correspondences are given below, in such a way that the average of approximately $365\frac{1}{4}$ days is preserved in the senatorial year, while at the same time the correspondence between the senatorial and the civil calendars in 432-1 is brought into harmony with the evidence of Thucydides as outlined on pp. 109-111.

I have also included in brackets the date of Pryt. I, 1, 411-0, because the regular succession of prytanies in the senatorial calendar was interrupted by the government of the Four Hundred. The unrestricted democracy was reëstablished, however, before the beginning of the following senatorial year, with the normal sequence of prytanies chosen as before. For the political changes during this period, *cf.* Ferguson, The Constitution of Theramenes, *Classical Philology,* XXI, 1926, pp. 72-75; also Chapter XI in the *Cambridge Ancient History,* Vol. V. These changes do not affect the validity of our reckoning of intercalary and ordinary years in the civil calendar from 411-0 to 407-6 as given above on pp. 94-100, nor do they affect the senatorial calendar except during 411-0 and the latter part of 412-1.

It will be noticed that our table of correspondences between the senatorial and the civil calendars brings Hek. 28 of the year 418-7 to the 32nd day of the first prytany. From *I.G.* I^2, 302, lines 4-5, we learn also that a payment was made to the hellenotamiae by the treasurers of Athena on this date, if in fact the date has been restored correctly. But I think it will be generally agreed that no payment could have been made on Hek. 28, the epochal date of the Panathenaic festival, and I suggest provisionally that the numeral in *I.G.* I^2, 302, lines 4-5, should be restored as δευτ[έραι καὶ εἰκοστῆι], bringing the date of the payment to the 22nd of the prytany, which corresponds to Hek. 18 in the civil calendar. In this case we may have an explanation for the elaborate transfers of money recorded in lines 5-8, for it is difficult to understand why the hellenotamiae should have to return to the treasurers the money received and then receive it again from them before passing it over to the generals in Thrace. If we suppose, however, that the original payment was made on Hek. 18, before the Panathenaic festival, we may assume that the decree of the senate and the assembly relative to the disposition of the money could not be put into effect until after the festival. Since the boards of hellenotamiae and treasurers changed office at the time of the festival, it was necessary for the money to be returned to the treasury before Hek. 28, so that the audit of both boards would be clear at the end of their term. When the new boards assumed their duties the money was again given for transfer to the generals in Thrace. The date of transfer recorded in the inscription, however, is the date of the original payment, for from that date began the reckoning of interest on the amount given as a loan to the Athenian state. We have already seen that in these records of money borrowed by the state the treasurers named in any given year are regularly those who entered office on Hek. 28, even though the payment may have fallen before this date, and the same lack of exactness in terminology may account for the failure here to distinguish between the two separate boards of hellenotamiae.

The revised tables of correspondences between the different calendars are given on the following pages.

118   THE ATHENIAN CALENDAR

Years of Metonic Cycle	Date of Attic Year	Julian Intercalation	Senatorial Year	Civil Year	Attic Intercalation	Correspondences between the Julian, senatorial, and civil calendars
—	434-3	I	366	354	O	July 3 — Pryt. I, 1 — Skir. 27 (435-4)
—	433-2	O	365	384	I	July 3 — Pryt. I, 1 — Hek. 9
1	432-1	O	365	354	O	July 3 — Pryt. I, 1 — Skir. 19 (433-2)
2	431-0	O	365	354	(O)	July 3 — Pryt. I, 1 — Hek. 1
3	430-29	I	366	384	(I)	July 3 — Pryt. I, 1 — Hek. 12
4	429-8	O	365	355	(O)	July 3 — Pryt. I, 1 — Skir. 24 (430-29)
5	428-7	O	365	384	(I)	July 3 — Pryt. I, 1 — Hek. 4
6	427-6	O	362	354	(O)	July 3 — Pryt. I, 1 — Skir. 14 (428-7)
7	426-5	I	366	384	I	June 30 — Pryt. I, 1 — Skir. 22 (427-6)
8	425-4	O	368	354	O	June 30 — Pryt. I, 1 — Skir. 5 (426-5)
9	424-3	O	365	355	O	July 3 — Pryt. I, 1 — Skir. 19 (425-4)
10	423-2	O	365	354	O	July 3 — Pryt. I, 1 — Skir. 29 (424-3)
11	422-1	I	366	384	I	July 3 — Pryt. I, 1 — Hek. 10
12	421-0	O	366	354	(O)	July 3 — Pryt. I, 1 — Skir. 21 (422-1)
13	420-19	O	366	354	(O)	July 4 — Pryt. I, 1 — Hek. 4
14	419-8	O	365	384	(I)	July 5 — Pryt. I, 1 — Hek. 16
15	418-7	I	366	384	(I)	July 5 — Pryt. I, 1 — Skir. 27 (419-8)
16	417-6	O	365	384	(I)	July 5 — Pryt. I, 1 — Skir. 8 (418-7)
17	416-5	O	365	355	(O)	July 5 — Pryt. I, 1 — Tha. 19 (417-6)
18	415-4	O	365	354	O	July 5 — Pryt. I, 1 — Tha. 29 (416-5)
19	414-3	I	366	384	I	July 5 — Pryt. I, 1 — Skir. 11 (415-4)
1	413-2	O	365	354	O	July 5 — Pryt. I, 1 — Tha. 22 (414-3)
2	412-1	O	365	354	O	July 5 — Pryt. I, 1 — Skir. 3 (413-2)
3	411-0	O	[366]	384	I	July 5 — [Pryt. I, 1] — Skir. 14 (412-1)
4	410-9	I	366	354	O	July 6 — Pryt. I, 1 — Tha. 26 (411-0)
5	409-8	O	366	355	O	July 6 — Pryt. I, 1 — Skir. 9 (410-9)
6	408-7	O	365	354	O	July 7 — Pryt. I, 1 — Skir. 20 (409-8)
7	407-6	O	365	355	O	July 7 — Pryt. I, 1 — Hek. 1
8	406-5	I	365	384	(I)	July 7 — Pryt. I, 1 — Hek. 11
9	405-4	O	365	354	(O)	July 6 — Pryt. I, 1 — Skir. 21 (406-5)
10	404-3	O	—	355	(O)	Period of Anarchy
11	403-2	O	—	384	(I)	and Restoration of the Democracy.
12	402-1	I	354	354	(O)	July 13 — Pryt. I, 1 — Hek. 1
13	401-0	O	384	384	(I)	July 1 — Pryt. I, 1 — Hek. 1

Attic Year	Dates of New Moons at the Beginning of the Civil Year, computed from Ginzel, *Handbuch der Chronologie*, Vol. I, Table III	Date of the Summer Solstice, as given by Ginzel, *op. cit.*, Vol. II, Table V, p. 578	
434-3	July 8 *c.* 4:13 A. M. Mean Athens Time	June 29	
433-2	June 26 *c.* 9:01 P. M. » » »	June 28	
432-1	July 15 *c.* 7:20 P. M. » » »	June 28	= June 27, according to ancient reckoning.
431-0	July 5 *c.* 3:59 A. M. » » »	June 28	*Cf.* Unger, in Mueller's
430-29	June 24 *c.* 6:23 A. M. » » »	June 29	*Handbuch*, Vol. I, p. 738.
429-8	July 11 *c.* 9:59 P. M. » » »	June 28	
428-7	July 1 *c.* 1:35 A. M. » » »	June 28	
427-6	July 19 *c.* 9:45 P. M. » » »	June 28	
426-5	July 9 *c.* 11:25 A. M. » » »	June 29	
425-4	July 27 *c.* 11:54 A. M. » » »	June 28	
424-3	July 17 *c.* 4:42 A. M. » » »	June 28	
423-2	July 6 *c.* 5:54 P. M. » » »	June 28	
422-1	June 26 *c.* 0:37 A. M. » » »	June 29	
421-0	July 13 *c.* 4:56 P. M. » » »	June 28	
420-19	July 2 *c.* 5:54 P. M. » » »	June 28	
419-8	June 21 *c.* 11:25 P. M. » » »	June 28	
418-7	July 10 *c.* 8:32 P. M. » » »	June 29	
417-6	July 28 *c.* 7:21 P. M. » » »	June 28	
416-5	August 16 *c.* 7:21 P. M. » » »	June 28	
415-4	August 6 *c.* 0:37 P. M. » » »	June 28	
414-3	July 27 *c.* 2:47 A. M. » » »	June 28	
413-2	August 14 *c.* 0:08 A. M. » » »	June 28	
412-1	August 3 *c.* 4:28 A. M. » » »	June 28	
411-0	July 23 *c.* 5:11 A. M. » » »	June 28	
410-9	August 10 *c.* 10:13 P. M. » » »	June 28	
409-8	July 30 *c.* 5:11 A. M. » » »	June 28	
408-7	July 19 *c.* 6:52 P. M. » » »	June 28	
407-6	July 9 *c.* 11:54 A. M. » » »	June 28	
406-5	June 29 *c.* 3:30 A. M. » » »	June 28	
405-4	July 17 *c.* 1:06 A. M. » » »	June 28	
404-3	July 6 *c.* 7:06 A. M. » » »	June 28	
403-2	June 25 *c.* 8:03 A. M. » » »	June 28	
402-1	July 14 *c.* 0:23 A. M. » » »	June 28	
401-0	July 2 *c.* 6:23 A. M. » » »	June 28	

Date of Hekatombaeon 1 by the Julian and Senatorial Calendars	First and Last Months of the Civil Year	Date of Attic Year
July 7 — Hek. 1 — Pryt. I, 5	Hek. 29 days — Skir. 30 days	434-3
June 25 — Hek. 1 — Pryt. X, 29-30 (434-3)	Hek. 29 days — Skir. 29 days	433-2
July 14 — Hek. 1 — Pryt. I, 12	Hek. 30 days — Skir. 29 days	432-1
July 3 — Hek. 1 — Pryt. I, 1	Hek. 30 days — Skir. 29 days	431-0
June 22 — Hek. 1 — Pryt. X, 26-27 (431-0)	Hek. 30 days — Skir. 30 days	430-29
July 10 — Hek. 1 — Pryt. I, 8	Hek. 29 days — Skir. 30 days	429-8
June 30 — Hek. 1 — Pryt. X, 34-35 (429-8)	Hek. 29 days — Skir. 29 days	428-7
July 19 — Hek. 1 — Pryt. I, 17	Hek. 30 days — Skir. 29 days	427-6
July 8 — Hek. 1 — Pryt. I, 9	Hek. 30 days — Skir. 30 days	426-5
July 26 — Hek. 1 — Pryt. I, 27	Hek. 29 days — Skir. 30 days	425-4
July 15 — Hek. 1 — Pryt. I, 13	Hek. 29 days — Skir. 30 days	424-3
July 5 — Hek. 1 — Pryt. I, 3	Hek. 29 days — Skir. 30 days	423-2
June 24 — Hek. 1 — Pryt. X, 28 (423-2)	Hek. 29 days — Skir. 29 days	422-1
July 12 — Hek. 1 — Pryt. I, 10	Hek. 30 days — Skir. 29 days	421-0
July 1 — Hek. 1 — Pryt. X, 34-35 (421-0)	Hek. 30 days — Skir. 29 days	420-19
June 20 — Hek. 1 — Pryt. X, 22-23 (420-19)	Hek. 30 days — Skir. 30 days	419-8
July 9 — Hek. 1 — Pryt. I, 5	Hek. 29 days — Skir. 29 days	418-7
July 27 — Hek. 1 — Pryt. I, 23	Hek. 30 days — Skir. 30 days	417-6
Aug. 15 — Hek. 1 — Pryt. II, 5-6	Hek. 29 days — Skir. 30 days	416-5
Aug. 5 — Hek. 1 — Pryt. I, 32	Hek. 29 days — Skir. 30 days	415-4
July 25 — Hek. 1 — Pryt. I, 21	Hek. 29 days — Skir. 29 days	414-3
Aug. 12 — Hek. 1 — Pryt. II, 2-3	Hek. 30 days — Skir. 29 days	413-2
Aug. 1 — Hek. 1 — Pryt. I, 28	Hek. 30 days — Skir. 29 days	412-1
July 21 — Hek. 1 — [Pryt. I, 17]	Hek. 30 days — Skir. 30 days	411-0
Aug. 9 — Hek. 1 — Pryt. I, 35	Hek. 29 days — Skir. 30 days	410-9
July 28 — Hek. 1 — Pryt. I, 23	Hek. 29 days — Skir. 30 days	409-8
July 18 — Hek. 1 — Pryt. I, 12	Hek. 29 days — Skir. 30 days	408-7
July 7 — Hek. 1 — Pryt. I, 1	Hek. 29 days — Skir. 30 days	407-6
June 27 — Hek. 1 — Pryt. X, 27-28 (407-6)	Hek. 29 days — Skir. 29 days	406-5
July 15 — Hek. 1 — Pryt. I, 10	Hek. 30 days — Skir. 29 days	405-4
July 4 — Hek. 1 Period of Anarchy	Hek. 30 days — Skir. 29 days	404-3
June 24 — Hek. 1 and Restoration of Democracy	Hek. 30 days — Skir. 30 days	403-2
July 13 — Hek. 1 — Pryt. I, 1	Hek. 29 days — Skir. 30 days	402-1
July 1 — Hek. 1 — Pryt. I, 1	Hek. 29 days — Skir. 29 days	401-0

Finally, we must consider the correspondence between the senatorial and civil calendars which appears in Antiphon's speech περὶ τοῦ χορευτοῦ, a correspondence which was used by Keil as the point of departure for his theory of the interrelation between the two calendar systems.

Here it is evident that in the year in which the speech was delivered:

1. Erechtheis held the first prytany, and the defendent had served as one of the prytanizing officers until the next to the last day of the prytany (§ 45; *cf.* also §§ 11 and 13).

2. The month of Hekatombaeon was full (30 days), and 20 days of Metageitnion had passed before the defendent was indicted (§ 44).

It was Maetzner's observation that the defendent had left the prytany because of the indictment, and Keil has drawn the logical conclusion that the next to the last day of the first prytany should be equated with the date of the indictment in the month of Metageitnion. The defendent claimed, however, that «more than fifty» days had elapsed since the beginning of the year during which time he had not been indicted (§ 44), and since the 30 days of Hekatombaeon and 20 days of Metageitnion do not add to give «more than fifty», Keil assumes that part of a numeral has fallen out of the text, and that instead of εἴκοσι we should read perhaps τρεῖς καὶ εἴκοσι or τρεῖς ἐπὶ εἴκοσι (*cf.* Keil, *Hermes,* XXIX, 1894, pp. 36-37). He equates the next to the last day of the prytany, therefore, with Metageitnion 22 or 23, eventually deciding in favor of the latter figure (*op. cit.,* p. 338).

Others have considered that the reading εἴκοσι is correct and that the words «more than fifty» are a rhetorical exaggeration. With the assumption that the first prytany contained 37 days, we may follow the latter suggestion and formulate the equation Pryt. I, 36 = Met. 21. Since the month of Hekatombaeon was full the equation may also be stated as Pryt. I, 1 = Hek. 16.

In the table given above on p. 118 we find that 419-8 is the only year in which this chronological correspondence existed, and in this year I propose that the speech must be dated. For literary history the determination is valuable as giving a fixed point for the study of the development of rhetorical style in Athens during the latter part of the Fifth Century.

We may note at this point that according to our table the beginning of the civil year falls occasionally near the new moon preceding the summer solstice, and occasionally near the second new moon following the summer solstice. The extremes of variation which I have given are, however, well attested. According to the tables Hek. 1 falls before the solstice in the following years: 433, 430, 422, 419, 406,

16

and 403. The time relation indicated for 433 is necessary, because we have proved that 433-2 was an intercalary year and because we know that Skir. 13 in 432 fell at the time of the solstice (p. 88). The first of Hekatombaeon in 433 must therefore have fallen before the solstice of 433. It would be possible to allow Hek. 1 in 430 to fall on the first new moon after the solstice by restoring 431-0 as an intercalary year and 430-29 as an ordinary year. I know of no way of deciding between this sequence and that proposed in the table, and I leave the question open. For the year 422 there is epigraphical proof that Hek. 1 fell before the solstice in the equation Pryt. I, 1=Hek. 10, derived from *I.G.* I², 324, line 79 (Plate II). The first day of the civil year must have fallen before the solstice in 419-8 in order to make possible the equation Pryt. I, 1 = Hek. 16, by which alone the speech of Antiphon περὶ τοῦ χορευτοῦ can be explained. The time relation as I have given it in 403 depends entirely on restoration, and there is no reason why 404-3 cannot be made an intercalary year, with 403-2 an ordinary year. In this case Hek. 1 of 403 would fall near the first new moon after the solstice.

Three times, however, during a period of 15 years (433-2 – 419-8), the first day of Hekatombaeon certainly fell before the summer solstice. I cannot believe that any very serious attempt was made to prevent this occurrence, although it may be noted that the beginning of the civil year never precedes the solstice by more than a few days.

On the other hand, the first day of the civil year might fall at the second new moon after the solstice. This is especially noticeable because of the irregularity of the extra intercalated month between 419-8 and 416-5. But this extra intercalation represents a true anomaly, and the irregularity was corrected by the omission of a month between 410-9 and 407-6. During the intervening years the fact of the irregularity is definitely proved by the correspondences between the civil and the senatorial calendars which appear in *I.G.* I², 328. It is impossible to allow Gamelion 7 and 25 of 414-3 to fall in Pryt. VII, without dating the first of Hekatombaeon in 413 at the second new moon after the solstice (*cf.* also pp. 93-94).

CHAPTER X

CONCLUSION

Until the discovery of further epigraphical evidence the inscription *I.G.* I², 324 must form the cornerstone of any study of the Athenian calendar in the Fifth Century, and the conclusions reached from a study of this inscription indicate the general lines on which any calendar system must be based. It is of especial importance that we now know the nature of the senatorial year, composed of ten prytanies of 36 and 37 days each, in such a way that the senatorial years average over a given period of time approximately $365\frac{1}{4}$ days, the equivalent of the actual solar year. Further evidence is needed before any comprehensive scheme of the civil calendar can be built up parallel to this senatorial calendar, for we know that the years of the Metonic cycle did not follow in any given sequence, and the calendar character of a year cannot be predicted merely by its position in the cycle. The consequences of this discovery in the first two Metonic cycles are far-reaching, and show that attempts to build up any calendar scheme merely by means of cycles of intercalation are destined to failure. This applies, for example, to Beloch's most recent chronological determinations for the interval between 338-7 and 206-5 B.C.[1], in so far as he has used a stereotyped sequence of years in the Metonic cycle in determining the dates of unassigned documents and the calendar character of individual years.

In our study of the Fifth Century, however, we have found that the senatorial year began about one week after the actual summer solstice, and so it is possible to reduce any date given in terms of the senatorial calendar to its approximate date in the Julian calendar without the intermediation of the civil year. Nor is the senatorial year subject to cycles or intercalation, and the reduction of dates to the Julian system of reckoning is relieved of a further complication which is always involved in

---

[1] Beloch, *Griechische Geschichte*, IV, 2², pp. 24 ff.

computations from the civil year. This method of reckoning may be carried back to the introduction of the ten tribes in the time of Kleisthenes, and it derives added importance from the fact that most of the dates throughout the fifth century are given in terms of the senatorial calendar.

There is no direct evidence as to the time when the senatorial year as we have described it above was abandoned in favor of the scheme outlined by Aristotle in which the senatorial and civil years were made of equal length. A study of the inscriptions from the latter part of the fourth century confirms the evidence of Aristotle, although it must be admitted that the prytanies vary in length sometimes during any given year from the canon as given in the *Constitution of Athens* (XLIII, 2). But it is not necessary to go into this problem here. The fact of the identity between the civil and senatorial years is sufficiently well attested for the latter part of the fourth century, and we may be certain that the change in the senatorial calendar took place at some time between 406-5 and, let us say, 341-0. The correspondences between dates by prytany and dates by civil month during the first half of the fourth century are too few and too indefinite to allow us to fix these provisional limits more closely.

But fortunately the solution of the problem does not depend on the discovery of corresponding dates. We have already observed (pp. 95 ff.) that the character of wording in official documents depends in part on whether the document in question was based on the senatorial year. We have seen, for example, that when such a year was to be dated exactly the phrase ἐπὶ τὲς βολὲς hὲι – –   *name* – – – πρõτος ἐγραμμάτευε was necessary. The senatorial year could not be dated exactly by the name of the eponymous archon of the civil year so long as the two years were not coterminous. This does not, however, preclude the possibility of dates in the fifth century given only by the name of the archon, even when the senatorial year was the year involved. The name of the archon was always convenient for use in dating and perfectly satisfactory when exactness was not required. We may find perhaps the best illustration of this phenomenon in the accounts of the overseers of work on two statues for the Hephaistion (*I.G.* I², 370). Exact dates are given only for those years where money was actually taken over from the Treasurers of the Other Gods. We find in 421-0, 420-19, and 418-7 the formula of date which reads as follows: ἐπὶ – – – *name* – – ἄρχοντος ἐπὶ τὲς βολὲς hὲι   – *name*   πρõτος ἐγραμμάτευε. The overseers held office during the senatorial year, and receipts were dated by prytany rather than by civil month (*I.G.* I², 370, line 6). But when no financial transactions were made, as in 419-8, 417-6, and 416-5, the exact terminology of dating as given above was not necessary, and we find the simple entries: ἐπὶ – – – *name* – – – ἄρχοντος οὐδὲν παρέλαβον. There was no need to define the year more closely.

Similarly, in the building accounts of the Erechtheum for the year 408-7 (*I.G.* I², 374) the date is given in the prescript merely by the name of the archon, although the accounts are clearly based on the senatorial year, which we know at this time not to have been coterminous with the civil year indicated by the name of the archon (*cf.* pp. 97-100).

I do not wish to imply that every document based on the senatorial calendar contained the date as indicated by the first secretary of the senate, but merely that when the exact definition of the senatorial year was required the name of the archon was not sufficient and that the phrase ἐπὶ τές βολές hέι – – – *name* – – – πρότος ἐγραμμάτευε was employed. It stood sometimes alone, sometimes in connection with the name of the archon. We have already observed that this formula was used in records of state expense. It appears also in the building accounts of the Parthenon (*I.G.* I², 339-353) and the Propylaea (*I.G.* I², 363-367) and in other records of expense and decrees as well.[1] But it was naturally less essential in a decree than in those records of receipt and expense which ran throughout the senatorial year.

Enough has been said, I believe, to indicate that this rather awkward formula was necessitated solely by the divergence between the civil and the senatorial years. When the phrase disappears from the inscriptions we may assume with considerable assurance that the dual nature of the Athenian calendar to which it owed its existence no longer obtained. I place the date of the change in the years of confusion at the close of the Peloponnesian war, and call attention to the fact that the formula for dating by the senatorial year as given above does not occur in the known inscriptions from the fourth century.[2] Dates given by the prytany still existed, for the year was still divided into ten periods during which the tribes held the prytany in turn. But the name of the archon was sufficient to designate the year correctly in the fourth century, whereas it had not been sufficient in the fifth century. The difference may be well illustrated by comparing the records of the ἐπιστάται at Eleusis for 421-0 (*I.G.* I², 311) with the records of the ἐπιστάται for 329-8 (*I.G.* II², 1672). In the record

---

[1] *I.G.* I², 52, 63, 310, 311, 358, 359, 368, 372. The formula is not always exactly the same, but the phrase τέι βολέι – – – *name* – – – πρότος ἐγραμμάτευε of the earlier Parthenon records has the same value. *Cf. I.G.* I², 340-348.

[2] When the permanent secretaryship was introduced at some time between 368 and 363 the name of the secretary indicated, in effect, the senatorial year. But I do not believe that this phenomenon has any connection with the change in character of the senatorial year.

from the fifth century we read: ἐπὶ τε͂ς βολε͂ς hε͂ι Πρέπις προ͂τος ἐγραμμάτευε ἐπὶ 'Αριστίονος ἄρχοντος etc., while in the fourth century we read merely: ἐπὶ Κηφισοφῶντος ἄρχοντος etc.

Public works and commissions elected to have charge of public works were also dated in the fourth century merely by the name of the eponymous archon. To my mind this implies that the year of the ten prytanies, which as representatives of the senate and the δῆμος had charge of the public works, was sufficiently well dated by the name of the archon. *Cf. I.G.* II², 1656, 1657, 1658, 1659, 1660, 1661, 1662, and 1663. The earliest of these inscriptions is dated in the year 395-4. We find also during the fourth century such references as ἡ βουλὴ ἡ ἐπ' 'Αγαθ[οκλέους ἄρχοντος] *I.G.* II², 124 (357-6), and ἡ βουλὴ ἡ ἐπὶ Πυθοδότου [ἄρχοντος] *I.G.* II², 223 (343-2). These quotations again imply the identity of the senatorial and civil years.

The occasion for the change from the old senatorial year to the new I believe to have been the year of the anarchy in 404-3 with the attendant lapse of older institutions. When democracy was reëstablished the senatorial year was made to conform to the civil year, and I assume that from 402 onward Pryt. I, 1 regularly coincided with Hek. 1. I have, in consequence, carried the table of correspondences between the old senatorial calendar of the fifth century and the civil calendar only so far as 405-4, the last significant date before the end of the Peloponnesian war and the fall of Athens.

BIBLIOGRAPHY*

I. ANCIENT AUTHORS AND TEXTS CITED.

ANTIPHON, Περὶ τοῦ χορευτοῦ.

ARISTOPHANES, *Clouds* and *Peace;* also scholia.

ARISTOTLE, *Constitution of Athens.*

      Meteorologica.

I(NSCRIPTIONES) G(RAECAE), Vol. I, *editio minor, ed.* F. Hiller von Gaertringen, Berlin, 1924, nos. 52, 63, 76, 81, 91, 110, 114, 193, 198, 220, 295-298, 302, 304, 306, 310, 311, 324, 328, 339-354, 358, 359, 363-367, 368, 370, 372, 374, 377.

I(NSCRIPTIONES) G(RAECAE), Vol. II and III, *editio minor, ed.* Johannes Kirchner, Berlin, 1913-1927, nos. 124, 223, 1656-1663, 1672.

PTOLEMY, *Almagest.*

THUCYDIDES.

II. MODERN AUTHORS.

BANNIER, W. De titulis aliquot atticis, *Diss.,* Berlin, 1891.

      Zu attischen Rechnungsurkunden des 5. Jahrhunderts, *Rheinisches Museum,* LXI, 1906, pp. 202-231, especially pp. 204-205.

      Zu griechischen Inschriften, *Rheinisches Museum,* LXX, 1915, pp. 411-415.

BELOCH, K. J. G. Griechische Geschichte, II, 2^2, pp. 228 ff., Strassburg, 1916.

      Griechische Geschichte, IV, 2^2, pp. 24 ff., Berlin, 1927.

BOECKH, AUG. Über zwei attische Rechnungsurkunden, *Kleine Schriften,* Vol. VI, pp. 72-138, especially pp. 89-138. (This paper was presented in 1846, and deals with fragments *a* and *b*).

      Über eine attische Rechnungsurkunde, *Kleine Schriften,* Vol. VI, pp. 211-251. (This paper was presented in 1853, and deals with fragments *f* and *e*).

---

* No attempt is made to give a complete bibliography of books and articles about the Athenian Calendar. I give here the titles of works to which reference is made in the text, together with some others which I have found useful for the study of the calendar in the fifth century.

Zur Geschichte der Mondcyclen der Hellenen, *Besonderer Abdruck aus den Jahrbüchern für classische Philologie,* Suppl. N. F. Bd. I, Heft 1 (1855).

Epigraphisch-chronologische Studien. Zweiter Beitrag zur Geschichte der Mondcyclen der Hellenen. *Besonderer Abdruck aus den Jahrbüchern für classische Philologie,* Suppl. N. F. Bd. II (1856).

CAVAIGNAC, E. Études sur l'Histoire Financière d'Athènes au Ve Siècle, Paris, 1908.

C(ORPUS) I(NSCRIPTIONUM) G(RAECARUM), Vol. I, *ed.* Aug. Boeckh, Berlin, 1828. *Cf.* no. 156 and *addenda,* p. 905 (publication of fragment *h*).

CURTIUS, C. Inschriften und Studien zur Geschichte von Samos, *Progr.,* Lübeck, 1877.

DIELS AND REHM, Parapegmenfragmente aus Milet, *Sitzungsberichte der Berliner Akademie,* 1904, pp. 92-101.

DITTENBERGER, W. *Cf.* Sylloge Inscriptionum Graecarum.

DODWELL, E. A Classical and Topographical Tour through Greece, Vol. I, London, 1819. (The first publication of fragment *h* is given on p. 372).

DROYSEN, J. G. Bemerkungen über die attischen Strategen, *Hermes,* IX, 1875, pp. 1-21, especially pp. 17-19.

FERGUSON, W. S. The Athenian Secretaries, *Cornell Studies in Classical Philology,* No. VII, 1898.

The Athenian Calendar, *Classical Philology,* III, 1908, pp. 386-398.

The Constitution of Theramenes, *Classical Philology,* XXI, 1926, pp. 72-75.

The Oligarchical Movement in Athens, *Cambridge Ancient History,* Vol. V, Chap. XI, 1927.

FOTHERINGHAM, J. K., Cleostratus, *Journal of Hellenic Studies,* XXXIX, 1919, pp. 164-184; XL, 1920, pp. 208-209; XLV, 1925, pp. 78-83.

The Metonic and Callippic Cycles, *Monthly Notices of the Royal Astronomical Society,* LXXXIV, 1924, pp. 383-392.

GINZEL, F. K. Handbuch der mathematischen und technischen Chronologie, Leipzig, 1906-1914, especially Vol. II (1911), chapter XI: Zeitrechnung der Griechen.

HAGGARD, P. The Secretaries of the Athenian Boule in the Fifth Century, *Transactions and Proceedings of the American Philological Association,* LVII, 1926, pp. XXXI-XXXII.

HERMANN, K. F. Über griechische Monatskunde, Göttingen, 1844.

HICKS, E. L. Greek Historical Inscriptions, Oxford, 1882 (*Cf.* no. 46).

HICKS, E. L. AND HILL, G. F. Greek Historical Inscriptions, Oxford, 1901 (*Cf.* no. 62).

I(NSCRIPTIONES) G(RAECAE), Vol. I, *ed.* A. Kirchhoff, Berlin, 1873 (*Cf.* no. 273, publication of fragments *a, b, c, d, e, f, g,* and *h*).

I(NSCRIPTIONES) G(RAECAE), Vol. I, *editio minor, ed.* F. Hiller von Gaertringen, Berlin, 1924. *Cf.* no. 324 (publication of fragments *a, b, c, d, e, f, g, h, i, k, l, m,* and *n,* edited by J. Kirchner. Fragment *o* is published separately by Hiller as no. 306).

KEIL, B. Attisches Viertelobolzeichen, *Hermes,* XXVII, 1892, pp. 643-647.

Athens Amtsjahre und Kalenderjahre im V. Jahrhundert, *Hermes,* XXIX, 1894, pp. 32-81.

Das System des Kleisthenischen Staatskalenders, *Hermes,* XXIX, 1894, pp. 321-372.

KIRCHHOFF, A. Bemerkungen zu den Urkunden der Schatzmeister der anderen Götter, *Abhandlungen der Berliner Akademie,* 1864.

KOERTE, A. Die Ausgrabungen am Westabhange der Akropolis IV, *Mitteilungen des deutschen archäologischen Instituts, Athenische Abteilung,* XXI, 1896, pp. 320-332.

Die Zeit des eleusinischen Zehntengesetzes, in NOACK, Eleusis, pp. 313-317.

KUBICKI, K. Das Schaltjahr in der grossen Rechnungs-Urkunde *I.G.* I², 273, *Progr.,* Ratibor, 1885 and 1888.

KUBITSCHEK, W. Grundriss der antiken Zeitrechnung, Munich, 1928.

MALTEZOS, K. Τὸ Ἀρχαῖον Ἀττικὸν Ἡμερολόγιον, Ἐφημερὶς Ἀρχαιολογική, 1907, pp. 239-244; 1908, pp. 143-150; 1908, pp. 284-314.

MERITT, B. D. AND WEST, A. B. The Reconstruction of *I.G.* I², 193, 194, and 201, *Transactions and Proceedings of the American Philological Association,* Vol. LVI, 1925, pp. 252-267.

A Revision of Athenian Tribute Lists, *Harvard Studies in Classical Philology,* XXXVII, 1926, pp. 55-98.

MICHEL, C. Recueil d'Inscriptions Grecques, Brussels, 1900 (*Cf.* no. 561).

MOMMSEN, A. Chronologie. Untersuchungen über das Kalenderwesen der Griechen, Leipzig, 1883.

Neuere Schriften über die attische Zeitrechnung, *Philologus,* 1902, pp. 201-244, especially pp. 214 ff.

Archonten und Schreiber in attischen Urkunden älterer Zeit, *Philologus,* 1903, pp. 348-356.

NICKLIN, T. The Attic Civil and Sacred Years, *Journal of Philology,* XXIV, 1896, pp. 54-82.

OPPERT, J. L'Année de Méton, *Revue des Études Grecques,* 1903, pp. 5-17.

PITTAKYS, K. S. *cf.* Ἐφημερὶς Ἀρχαιολογική, 1853, nos. 1204 (fragment *f*) and 1204 δίς, p. 830 (fragment *f*), no. 1351 (fragment *e*); 1854, no. 2189 (fragment *c*), nos. 2266, 2267 fragments *a* and *b*); Ἀρχαιολογικὴ Ἐφημερίς, δευτέρα περίοδος, 1862, no. 115 (fragment *d*).

RANGABÉ, A. R. *cf.* Ἐφημερὶς Ἀρχαιολογική, 1837, no. 20 (fragment *b*); 1839, no. 259 (fragment *a*).

Antiquités Helléniques, Vol. I, Athens, 1842. *Cf.* nos. 116 and 117 (fragments *a* and *b*).

Antiquités Helléniques, Vol. II, Athens, 1855. *Cf.* nos. 373 and 2253 *b* (fragment *e*), no. 2253 *a* (fragment *f*).

Lettre adressée a M. de Saulcy, *Revue Archéologique,* 1845, pp. 321-337, especially pp. 323-324 (fragment *e*).

ROBERTS, E. S. AND GARDNER, E. A. An Introduction to Greek Epigraphy, Part II: The Inscriptions of Attica, Cambridge, 1905 (*Cf.* no. 109).

SCHMIDT, A. Handbuch der griechischen Chronologie, Jena, 1888.

S(UPPLEMENTUM) E(PIGRAPHICUM) G(RAECUM), Vol. II, 1925, no. 3.

S(YLLOGE) I(NSCRIPTIONUM) G(RAECARUM), *ed.* W. Dittenberger, Leipzig, 1883. *Cf.* no. 29.

TANNER, R. The Δραπέτιδες of Cratinus and the Eleusinian Tax Decree, *Classical Philology,* XI, 1916, pp. 65-94.

UNGER, G. F. Der attische Kalender während des pelop. Krieges, *Sitzungsberichte der Münchner Akademie,* 1875, Vol. II, pp. 53 ff.

Review of Kubicki, *op. cit., Berliner Philologische Wochenschrift,* 1888, pp. 1572-1576.

Griechische Zeitrechnung, in Mueller's *Handbuch der klassischen Altertums-Wissenschaft,* Vol. I², pp. 715-778.

Die Zinsurkunde zu Ol. 88,3 - 89,2 (CIA. I 273), *Neue Jahrbücher für Philologie und Pedagogik,* 1893, pp. 225-260.

USENER, H. Chronologische Beiträge, *Rhein. Museum,* XXXIV, 1879, pp. 388-441. [Reprinted in Usener's *Kleine Schriften,* Vol. III, pp. 472-531]

WEST, A. B. The Chronology of the Years 432 and 431 B.C., *Classical Philology,* 1915, pp. 34-53.

Notes on Payments made by the Treasurers of Athena in 416-5 B.C., *American Journal of Archaeology,* XXIX, 1925, pp. 3-16.

WEST, A. B. ΚΑΙ MERITT, B. D. Ὁ Φορολογικὸς Κατάλογος τοῦ 421-0, Ἀρχαιολογικὴ Ἐφημερίς, 1924, pp. 41-49.

Cleon's Amphipolitan Campaign and the Assessment List of 421, *American Journal of Archaeology,* XXIX, 1925, pp. 59-69.

DESCRIPTION OF PLATES

PLATE I

The facsimile reproduction of *I. G.* I², 324 was made with the help of squeezes on which the letters were drawn over in heavy black. These were then traced onto drawing paper in India ink. This copy was compared with the original and, after correction, was photographed onto zinc-line plates by the photo-engraver's process. The scale of the reproduction is one third natural size (1 : 3).

Those parts of the inscription which are still preserved, or which have been seen by earlier editors, are given in black. The restorations are in red. The designation of the various fragments is indicated by letters along the margin. Fragment *h* has been lost and is known to us only from Dodwell's copy (*cf.* Bibliography). Portions of fragment *e* have also been lost since its first publication. The inner circumscribing line gives the size of the fragment as it is preserved today; the outer circumscribing line includes those pieces which have been broken away since the fragment was discovered.

PLATE II

This plate gives in transcript the restored text of the inscription. No attempt has been made to preserve the *stoichedon* order of the letters, which is sufficiently well indicated in Plate I. The usual conventions of epigraphical text have been observed, except that words broken at the end of a line have not been hyphenated.

INDEX

Brasidas, Spartan general in Thrace, 114; Truce of, 87, 111.

Charopides, Plates, line 27.

Civil year, composition of in 423-2, 77; definition of, 4; relation of commencement of to solar year 121, 122.

Cleon, connection with the affair at Pylos, 91; death of, 114; proposal to double the tribute, 26, 92.

Clouds of Aristophanes and complaints about the calendar, 104, 105.

Comet in January of 426 B. C., 92-93.

Corcyra, Athenian expedition to in 433, 85.

Cross-references between the civil and senatorial years, in 422, 84; in 419, 121; in 411, 84; in 407, 97.

Dates of payments from Athena's money in tabular form, 70-71.

Dating by year, methods of, 16, 95.

Demetrios, first secretary of the senate in 423-2, 8, 78, 79, Plates, lines 37, 57.

Demophon, 22, 23, Plates, lines 70, 87.

Demosthenes, connection with the affair at Pylos, 91, 92, Plates, line 18.

Diodorus (XII, 36), reference to Meton's cycle, 88, 102.

Dionysus, 22, Plates, line 81.

Eclipses, of moon (Oct. 9, 425), 89, 90, 92; of moon, mentioned by Ptolemy (383-2 and 382-1), 107; of sun (Aug. 3, 431), 104.

Epilykos, first secretary of the senate in 424-3, 18, 26, Plates, line 26.

Ἐπιστάται at Eleusis, records of, 125.

Erechtheum, building accounts, 100, 125; excavations in, 3.

Eurymedon, general at Pylos, 91.

Euthias, secretary of the treasurers of the sacred moneys of Athena in 433-2, 86.

Foreign God, 22, Plates, line 86.

Four Hundred, interruption of the senatorial calendar under, 116-117.

Fractions, difficulty of computation of, 32, 33, 35.

Fragments of *I.G.* I², 324, (*a*) 4, 25; (*b*) 4, 25; (*c*) 4, 25; (*d*) 4, 20 (photograph), 23; (*e*) 4; (*f*) 4, 20, 23, 25; (*g*) 4; (*h*) 4, 83; (*i*) 4, 5, 6 (photograph); (*k*) 4, 21 (photograph), 23, 24; (*l*) 4, 5, 6 (photograph); (*m*) 4, 7, 8 (photograph); (*n*) 4, 6, 7 (photograph), 8, 23, 24; (*o*) 4, 6, 7 (photograph), 8; (*p*) 4, 24 (photograph).

Gorgoinos, treasurer of the Other Gods in 423-2, 24, 74, 75, 77, 79, Plates, lines 55, 76, 77, 94, 96.

He-(?), one of the Other Gods, 22, Plates, line 70.

Hekatombaeon, intercalation of, 105.

Hellenotamiae, payments made to, 18, 79, 111, 117; term of office, 19.

Hephaestus, 22; payment from treasure of with interest accrued, 13, Plates, line 85.

Herakles in Kynosarges, 22, 80, Plates, line 69; second payment from the treasure of and interest accrued, 13, Plates, line 87.

Hermes, 3, 49, 82, Plates, lines 109-111.

Hiller von Gaertringen, restorations in *I.G.* I², 63, 90.

Hippokrates, general in 426-5, Plates, line 3.

Hippolyteion, *cf.* Aphrodite by the Hippolyteion.

Ilissus, 22; second payment from the treasure of in 423-2, 28, Plates, line 84.

Intercalary years, evidence for, in 433-2, 88; in 426-5, 92-93; in 422-1, 101-114; in 415-4 or 414-3, 93-94; in 411-0, 94.